D1045178

DISCARD

DATE			

◻ DEDICATION ◻

To
Mom and Dad
whose embrace gave me life
and to
Norman Vincent Peale
whose arms introduced me to the
loving embrace of God

CONTENTS

1.
GOD'S LOVING EMBRACE 11

2.
PIECES OF DREAMS 20

3.
GOD'S EVIDENT TOUCH 40

4.
THE EMBRACE THAT BINDS 47

5.
OF BIRDS, BLOSSOMS, AND BUTTERFLIES 65

6.
EMBRACE FAITH AND BE STRONG 87

7.
POWER FOR LIVING IN GOD'S EMBRACE 103

8.

GOD'S LOVE NEVER FAILS 109

9.

THE EMBRACE OF GRACE 116

10.

FAITH MAKES
YOU CONFIDENT 125

11.

THE EMBRACEABLE
LOOK OF LOVE 137

12.

THE HEART EXCHANGE 153

13.

GOD, CAN WE TALK? 164

14.

LET YOUR EMBRACE BRIDGE
OTHERS TO CHRIST 183

15.

NO GRAVE DOUBTS
ABOUT EASTER 206

EPILOGUE 217

NOTES 219

My God, I love Thee,
Not because I hope for heav'n thereby,
Nor yet because who love Thee not
Must die eternally.
Thou, O my Jesus,
Thou didst me upon the cross *embrace,*
For me didst bear the nails and spear
And manifold disgrace.
Why, then why, O blessed Jesus Christ,
Should I not love Thee well?
Not for the hope of winning heav'n
Or of escaping hell;
Not with the hope of gaining aught,
Not seeking a reward;
But as Thyself hast loved me,
O everloving Lord!
E'en so I love Thee,
And will love,
And in Thy praise will sing;
Solely because
Thou art my God,
And my Eternal King.

Jane M. Marshall
My Eternal King
Carl Fisher Music Co.
Used by permission

GOD'S LOVING EMBRACE

CHAPTER 1

God's Loving Embrace

*D*ear God . . ."

Her letter said it all. Two days before she died in a tragic fire, nine-year-old Alice Latasha Shedrick wrote an essay for her fourth-grade class about her best friend—God.

In this composition she expressed her love for him. This child knew the loving embrace of God. A photograph of her letter appeared on the front page of the *New York Daily News* with the bold caption "My Best Friend."

> My best friend is God. He is my father. Without him I wouldn't be born. Everybody has something to thank God for. Their eyes, hands, ears, nose, legs and life.
>
> God is always there when I need someone to talk to. When something is going wrong for me, God will help me out and he will show me the right way.
>
> I thank God for giving the life he has given me. I think that everyone who has had troubles should ask God for forgiveness and we should all love him and I want to go in his big house in the sky.

Millions of New Yorkers, and Americans around the

country, were touched by little Alice. She gripped the hearts of many people as she expressed a simple love for God.

It was a poignant letter, simply expressing the loving embrace that God has for all his children. In her childhood, Alice expressed what so many people have a hard time articulating or discovering: the joyous love of God as our friend.

Two days after Alice submitted this assignment to her teacher, she did go to "his big house in the sky." A major New York City fire took her life.

Everyone believed that such a perfect, simple, and trusting faith would provide her with the loving embrace of God.

Hers was a letter for all people. It is this same message of love which I desire to share with you so that you might discover in that loving embrace your greatest friend—God!

The moment was almost absolutely silent.

Stillness was suspended within the room, interrupted only by the peculiarly penetrating rays of light breaking through the stained-glass windows like a spectacular morning sunrise.

Something was wonderfully different. The miracle unfolding before our very eyes was indescribably beautiful and precious. In silence and stillness, joy began its movement.

It was the Christmas season. All was calm and still. All was bright. Comfort and joy were mysteriously touching all of us as a canopy overhead, embracing us with God's love.

It was winter and Christmas, yet all was far from wintry bare and lifeless. In the life of one man before us were captured the bright starry skies of heaven. Their radiant splendor touched each of our lives. We were watching a miracle unfold.

Peace pulsed from the life of one who stood before my congregation, committing his life to God, his friend and his new-found hope, his assurance that he was loved. An aura of splendor, beauty, and contentment soothed his once tormented anguish.

For the first time in months, his troubled life found solace and healing in the loving embrace of God.

The carol *Silent Night* had new meaning for all of us. Peace was God's ultimate blessing for Martin. It was a gift given by God to restore the confidence and hope he so desperately needed.

Faith had eluded him during his life and most recently in the tragedy he had endured. Confidence and hope were overshadowed by despair, pain, and stress. They had escaped him because of his inability or unwillingness to give his life to God.

But we were watching God's strong embrace engulf him in love because a little child led him to this moment of faith that would forever change his life.

With my hands gently resting upon his head, Martin Aquaah received the blessing of God. He was joining the church. He had found in God a close friend, a Lord, a Savior. His new hope for abundant life would pull his splintered life together.

"Martin, the Lord is with you! The grace of our Lord Jesus Christ is with you always!"

These words of hope assured him that he would, from this moment on, be aware of the truth that he was held in the loving embrace of God. Martin was discovering God as his best friend. What he was now acknowledging was that God had always been there for him. He had now chosen to accept God in his life.

A little child led her father to this loving embrace. Martin had walked through the deepest valley of darkness into the gentle, sustaining hands of God. A nine-year-old girl changed her father's life.

Martin's eyes reflected the bright stars of hope. They mirrored the twinkling spectacle of white lights adorning the Christmas tree, its gleams captured in the glistening tears of a man who felt deeply the encouraging embrace of God's love.

Below his bowed head, the dark, shining skin of Martin, African by birth, was aglow with the presence of light. Brightness and joy ricocheted from his cheekbones, spreading a warmth to all around him. Surely the Lord was in this place. We saw Him in Martin's life. We felt Him moving among us. Our lives were brushed by the hush of angel wings.

I stood in amazement, contemplating and understanding God's healing love provided through His loving touch. Martin's life testified to the miracle that lives are daily changed and renewed, restored and made radiantly vibrant, by the embrace of a loving God who leads us to wholeness.

This was a day of joy for Martin. Just a short time ago, his life was shattered by tragedy. Now his life revealed the resiliency of the human spirit when God is present.

In submission to God, he lowered his head to receive the benediction that would seal his unshakable faith. "Now may the Lord be with you."

And He was.

God had led this man through his darkest valley. This day they began journeying through life with hands linked and hearts fused.

During this precious moment I saw the powerful influence of God. It was brightly evident as diamond facets on fire with light. I had seen many glorious sights in nature, but none to equal this solemn and splendid moment of miracle and mystery. God was embracing Martin Aquaah.

At this moment I was transported back to an earlier time when Martin's head was lowered. He was a broken man, languishing over the tragedy of his daughter's horrifying death. His head was bowed in pain.

Only eight short months before this Christmas season, Bertha, Martin's vivacious nine-year-old daughter, led the Sunday school children in the triumphant procession of palms during the Palm Sunday worship celebration.

The congregation thrilled to the sounds of children's voices singing,

Hosanna, loud Hosanna the little children sang;
Through pillared court and temple the lovely anthem rang.
To Jesus, who had blessed them
Close folded to His breast,
The children sang their praises, the simplest and the best.

We were proud of these children, especially little Bertha, as she led the enthusiastic Sunday school down the center aisle with flowing, waving fanned green palm branches. The children's faces expressed our praise and honor to God, our thanksgiving for His loving embrace in our lives.

After church that Sunday, Bertha excitedly entered my office and asked if she could use the phone to call home. "I have to let my daddy know to pick me up!" Martin never attended church, never entered our facility. The closest he ever came was in a car to pick up his daughter after Sunday school and church. Bertha loved God. Martin did not know Him.

On Tuesday of Holy Week, the church office received a hysterical and horrifying phone call from the superintendent of Bertha's apartment building to inform us that she had been missing for a few days. Her battered, abused body was discovered in a black, plastic Hefty garbage bag in a local park along the Hudson River.

Our inner-city church was thrust once again into the harsh reality of the dark side of urban life.

Bertha's stepmother had beaten her unconscious and then placed this battered child in the kitchen oven. Setting the dial on broil, the demented woman burned the child beyond recognition.

The stepmother was jealous of Martin's devoted love for little Bertha.

In Holy Week I stood with Martin in the kitchen of his apartment. There, in the room where the unfathomable happened to his child, he stood crushed and hopeless. There we embraced each other in quiet numbness, waiting to hear the silence speak comfort to us.

The moment echoed no peace, no calm, no joy. The light of his life had been extinguished.

Only our loving embrace, in front of the stove, as we sat at the kitchen table, spoke to us. Martin found comfort in the corner of my shoulder. I struggled to share a silent prayer of hope that God might penetrate his mind with calming peace.

Painfully and hesitantly, Martin lowered the oven door.

As his hand reached for the handle, my own deep horror at his faltering movement made me want to restrain him from confronting the horrible site where his daughter had lost her life. The scene was awesome. Just the day before one human being had taken the life of another. A child. His child.

But this tragedy would lead Bertha's daddy into the loving embrace of God.

Peering into the black emptiness within the oven, I could not help but consider what God must have thought as He saw the loathsome, frightful, and shocking murder of Bertha.

Then, as I moved beyond my aversion, my social consciousness was also raised.

What did God think and feel as He observed the ovens at Auschwitz?

What does God feel as He looks down upon the oppressed children of apartheid?

What pain is thrust into the heart of God as He feels the emptiness of the stomachs of His starving children throughout the world?

What empathy and compassion are generated from this God who watches homeless victims and aimless drifters huddled for warmth on the subway air vent grills on city streets?

Where is this God who is so desperately needed by people seeking the comfort of a compassionate embrace, the assurance of a guiding hand? Is He nowhere to be found?

Anger gripped me when I began asking, "Where were you, God, when little Bertha Aquaah was being murdered by her stepmother? This should never have happened!"

As if my opinion would have altered or manipulated the outcome of the event. What audacity in holding God accountable. "Why did He not intervene on behalf of this defenseless child?"

A story told by Elie Wiesel, recipient of the Nobel peace prize provided me with my answer. It captures the way God's loving embrace reaches down and does, in fact, intervene within the lives of people. It is an embrace often disguised by life's harsh realities. Nonetheless, God directly participates.

As Wiesel tells of his imprisonment in a concentration camp, he presents a horrifying moment in which he is watching three individuals being led to the gallows, blindfolded and prepared for hanging. He overhears one in the crowd gathered to observe this degrading spectacle say, "Where is God?"

Two of the three being hung are men. One is a teenage boy. As the trap doors are opened and the three drop to the snapping sounds of the ropes around their necks, the two men die rather quickly.

But not so the young boy, whose emaciated body hangs almost weightless in the air. He dangles for almost half an hour before his body gives way to suffocation.

Again from the crowd the cry is lifted up: "Where is God?!!"

"Where is God?!"

A man behind Elie Wiesel turns and says, "Where is God? Why, He is there! Hanging on the gallows!"

God intercedes for humanity, suffering and hurting along with His children. God Himself suffered on the gallows.

And God was present at little Bertha's darkest hour. He intervenes in our needs. His loving embrace sustains us through life's greatest trials, deepest hurts, and sharpest unfulfilled longings.

In this darkest hour, God was leading Martin Aquaah to the pathway of peace.

The Aquaah family could not afford the full funeral expenses. The church helped them to meet the exorbitant costs.

Throngs of people gathered at the funeral home for services rich in African tradition. In colorful African dress, family and friends gathered. They sang praise to God in their native language. The room was filled with much grief—and with intense hope.

The memorial service that followed at church led Martin for the first time into the place of worship his little girl had grown to love.

Now, eight months later Bertha's father was committing his life to God.

Martin expressed his love to our congregation by affirming the joy of the Christmas season.

"A little child led me to church!" he said.

His precious little girl, Bertha.

Before he turned to receive my hands of blessing upon his head he said, "How could a church pay for the funeral of my daughter, when her father had no time for God? How could they show so much love to a father who had no time for God, who had no interest in God or faith, and who had no intention of ever joining the fellowship and life of this congregation?

"I am joining this church, affirming my faith in God as my Lord and Savior, not because a church paid for my daughter's funeral expenses. I am committing my life to God because a little child, my daughter, led me to the place where I found the loving embrace of God.

"Bertha knew God's love here. Now God is loving me here. You have loved me here."

Martin's life was now centered in the loving embrace of God. God's hand moved in his life with healing and wholeness. The miracle was transcendent in its grandeur and in its message. With the feeble powers of our finite imaginations, we watched the unfolding of God's will. Before us a miracle transpired.

This was a special Christmas for all of us. A little child had led Martin Aquaah to this moment when God revealed His ability to hold each of our lives in His loving embrace.

A little child born in a manger continues to lead our lives into that same loving embrace.

In that embrace we discover the promise of comfort and joy, hope and peace. This God gives us peace always, in every way, for all of our needs.

The congregation rose up to their feet singing in triumphant faith:

> Hail the heaven-born Prince of Peace!
> Hail the Sun of Righteousness!
> Light and life to all he brings,
> Risen with healing in his wings,
> Mild he lays his glory by,
> Born that man no more may die,
> Born to raise the sons of earth,
> Born to give them second birth.
> Hark! the herald angels sing,
> "Glory to the Newborn King."

This God's loving hands would become more evident in my own life, sustaining me in my deepest and darkest time.

For as my hands were placed upon Martin's head, evoking the peace and blessing of God, I was yearning for myself, to feel that significant touch that could change and remake me.

I was going through one of life's darkest moments. I yearned for God's evident hand within my life. Martin stood before me whole.

I was standing before him, my congregation, and God, broken.

I was the one who needed a second birth!

CHAPTER 2

Pieces of Dreams

How much do you tell about yourself in a book that is read by a broad spectrum of the population? Does exposing one's soul invite staring eyes and curious minds into private rooms that should remain closed to inquisitive, and often nosy, thrill seekers? If a story is to be credible, honest, substantiated by growth and vulnerability, can a writer engrave across the outward facade of his life the words, "No admittance!" "Private!" "Keep Out!" "No trespassing"? We can conveniently do what department stores do when they change seasonal window displays. Pull down a shade, over which is written in attractive calligraphy, "Pardon our appearance while we are changing." We remain curious about what is concealed behind the scenes, never seeing the labor shuttered behind the veil, but only the window dressing, illusionary yet captivating and appealing. Should we be seen only as a finished product, or can we risk being seen as a person in formation? Honestly and openly?

Some window designers enter their stores after business hours and work throughout the night. The waking world, catching a first glimpse of the new ornamentations, is virtually unconscious that a change has taken place, or if indeed it has, asks, "When did it happen?"

20

In January I attended the 1990 Boat Show, one of the largest displays of power and sailboats in America, held at the Jacob Javits Center on the west side of New York City at the Hudson River and 34th Street. Thousands of boats, hundreds of dealers, yet in the weeks before the Boat Show opening on January 13, with all of my trips to midtown Manhattan, I did not see one yacht or sail, no trailers being guided through some of the narrow city streets in the midtown vicinity of the Javits Center. Yet the convention center doors swung open to a spectacular display of the world of boating. Each vendor proclaimed, "We've Got the Look" and offered "a vacation like no other!" Boats were diverse enough to match the daydreams of those who wish to sail yachts or cruise on the luxuriously equipped power fleet. And everything in between. Each bow to stern seemed to be covered with those seeking to fulfill a dream. "Upgrade," was the encouraging advice given by all sales personnel. "Where do you boat? Are you ready to upgrade!" It was the kind of show where the "green-eyed monster roams" conspicuously!

One of the reasons, however, that I did not see the transport of boats along city streets, to the convention center, is that I rarely was in the vicinity of the Javits Center. It is like positioning yourself on a parade route, without going to the site of its origin, where all the hard work is done in preparation for the cavalcade. You see the pagentry of floats and the Thanksgiving Day traditional balloons of Popeye, Bullwinkle, Spiderman suspended along Broadway, without having seen the hours of pre-dawn effort to inflate these cartoon legends.

Do those of us who speak from public platforms, from pulpits, often convey a message which is only a tailored product, a finely tuned oratorical statement or a deeply inspiring devotional, prophetic, or pastoral message, without introducing anyone to the inner change, growth, stretching, struggle, and pain of the soul's journey in its formation of the one who stands before those listening ears? Orators deliver a message about changing lives without ever exposing that God has broken their own clay feet and remolded them into wholeness and completeness. The writer or speaker often draws the shades and assumes that others know there are changes going on. Or that some would rather not become aware of the flaws in those they hold in high esteem.

Can a writer fashion a complete story without lifting the shade so that others might know of the process that results in deeper growth and forming wholeness? If a story is to be credible there must be a tilting of the blinds to allow a glance into the process so that what is displayed does not eventually appear illusionary but substantial. Yet rarely do you see mannequins stripped to their flesh-toned, plaster forms in store windows. There is respect, order, and fashion in the way creative displays are originated. Neither should we require of ourselves to be stripped to the bare soul for the speculation, curiosity, and perverted innuendos of thrill seekers. Human beings like gossip. Why should one cultivate soils in which it can germinate more easily?

A national comedienne said about Jimmy the Greek's removal from television, "What happens when you tell the truth on a national broadcasting system? You're gone!" This is why many fear to tell the story of their inner journey. If you do, you're gone.

The public forum is not a confessional. The throne of grace is where the repentant heart brings its fervent prayer and its shattered self to the embrace of God. Too often the general public does not understand the growth process and will leave you a shattered person, if not splintering you even further. Somewhere in between, however, the story, if it is to lead others to the grace of God, must convey the rough mountain climbing and the wandering, desolate valley or desert journey. The blights and the blessings must both be part of the story telling. The scriptural injunction is emphatic: "Where sin abounded, grace abounded much more."[1]

The emphasis must be on the grace, simply because there is more of it. It takes precedence in God's intention with us. He forgets our sins, but He does not forget His benefits.

When I attended my first writer's workshop as a novice, an aspiring young writer, Word Publishing Company out of Waco, Texas, raised my anxiety level rather than unleashing my enthusiasm with the comment, "So, you want to write!? Well, be ready to be criticized!" The revelations of your personal life in print will teach you the agility to dodge the darts as well as affirm you as you taste the triumphs. The transparency of your life will solicit criticism as well as affirmation of your honesty, which liberates others to face themselves. Jesus will always serve as the "shield and defender." If my writing, life, honesty, and vulnerability can bring Him worship and glory, if it will help others in their struggle to grow and to change, then I pray that God will use these words as strength for the inward journey to self-discovery and the disclosure of God's loving embrace within the hearts of hurting people.

I do not want to offer to people pieces only of His promises. Nor do I want to offer them a piece of myself, a portion of my journey. Much of my life has been joy-filled and successful. A portion of it has been dismal and humiliating. In fact, much of it has hurt my soul and saddened the spirit of God. From boyhood on I sang a hymn that wove itself into my faith fabric: "O Jesus, I have promised / To serve thee to the end." But then I discovered that He was recipient of only "pieces of that promise." Even with my own wife, I discovered this to be true. When I married her we exchanged the traditional vows that said, "Will you promise to love and cherish?" I loved her. But I didn't cherish the love! As a result, she received only a piece of the promise, so the promise broke into shattered pieces.

The last sentence of my first chapter lifts the shades, opens the blinds, and conveys to you that within the binding of this book are chapters of a life that has been complex and confused, frightened and alone, broken and shattered, abandoned and isolated, and far from honest in its introspection as well as a life that has been comforted and encouraged, graced and loved, hugged and affirmed, set free and lifted high, picked up and set on its feet, guided down right paths along which I met many who, in spite of knowing all about me, committed themselves to walking with me until I arrived home. They waited and watched until I unlocked the door to my heart, until they saw the light turned on within and acknowledged that I was safely in refuge. Their steadfast love and God's grace became mortar for my brokenness.

This book is written so that all who read it might find the comfort that comes with peace and grace at home within your lives. Within each person who walked with me, I saw Jesus Christ, Himself. This is the full promise I wish to share. No one deserves just a piece of that promise.

Thomas Merton in his book *No Man Is an Island* helped me realize two things: the need to risk self in telling the story so that the words do not remain empty and only fragments of the promise; and the need to be aware that some can abuse, confuse, misuse, and refuse to hear what you have to say.

Merton says, "If our life is poured out in useless words, we will never hear anything in the depths of our hearts, where Christ lives and speaks in silence. We will never be anything, and in the end, when the time comes for us to declare who and what we are, we shall be found speechless at the moment of the crucial decision: for we shall have said everything and exhausted ourselves in speech before we had anything to say."[2]

For this book not to echo empty words, but to resonate the gospel's truth, its credibility must be seen in the truth of an unveiled window display to allow the reader, as well as the writer, to see his path of growth, humbly raising the shades and revealing the shadows so that God's light, mercy, and grace are fully known. The question asked in this book is perhaps the same one asked of me as I roamed the floors at the Boat Show in the Javits Center. "Do you want to upgrade?" Do you want to grow? Do you want to change your life?" It is not a question about acquiring larger yachts or more successful lives. It is a question about humbly asking the Lord to step into your boat, your life, so that your soul might become whole, your heart complete, and your joy abundant.

David Eisenhower and his wife Julie Nixon were visiting my summer home in Ocean Grove, New Jersey, and I invited a few family friends to have a time of fellowship with the Eisenhowers. During our informal gathering and conversation I asked David an intentional question, one loaded with speculation about his future political goals and dreams as a way of making him feel somewhat more comfortable around the newfound friends gathered to greet the couple.

"Dave, what are your aspirations for the future?" I asked, quite confident that the question would give him the arena to talk about his life, his career goals and dreams.

"My aspirations for the future, Ron! Well, I'm living those aspirations now!" David responded. His response still resonates in my ears. David taught me a deeply needed lesson at that moment in my life. "Live life fully now, thoroughly confident that as you aspire to live wholly and completely in the moment, you are constantly aspiring to a nobler essence of life in the moment."

Another friend, Bill Stark, recuperating in Columbia Presbyterian Hospital in New York City, discussed his surgery with me when I visited him after a rather difficult surgical procedure. After listening to him share his fears, anxieties, and unwavering confidence in God's guidance and comfort, he switched the conversation to me.

"How's your life going?" he inquired.

"Well," I said. "Career is blossoming, church is growing, on the threshold of publishing several books."

"Oh, I'm not concerned about your career," he said. "How's your walk with the Lord?"

I was stunned to a moment of silence.

Forthrightly confronted by the essential question. Two responses, one from David Eisenhower, the other from Bill Stark, about how whole and meaningful life should be. Their comments dovetailed, hitting me squarely between the eyes of my faith, which had become dimmed by my speculation about my future, a future I was certain was one in which God was calling me to do great things. But first I needed to learn, in a more intentional way, to "aspire to a closer walk with the Lord—now!"

Thomas Merton said, "Secrecy and solitude are values that belong to the very essence of personality. A person is a person insofar as he has a secret and has solitude of his own that cannot be communicated to anyone else. If I love a person, I will love that which most makes him a person: the secrecy, the hiddenness, the solitude of his own individual being, which God alone can penetrate and understand. A love that breaks into the spiritual privacy of another in order to lay open all his secrets and besiege his solitude with importunity does not love him: it seeks to destroy what is best in him, and what is most intimately his."[3]

When you share your life in a book, you move away some of the comforting, assuring confines of solitude. People see inside of you. Certainly we know from Scripture that no secrets are hidden from God. As our creator He is willing to work with us so that our lives achieve His very likeness. He does this by pardoning our sins so that our appearance may be like His.

Inviting others into the inner spiritual privacy of my own life has intentionally challenged me to lead them, not necessarily into my story, but into the gospel story. The hymn "May The Mind of Christ My Savior" undergirds my desire for people to see not only my growth and struggle but primarily God's grace central to the journey. "May His beauty rest upon me as I seek the lost to win, And may they forget the channel, seeing only Him."

First Corinthians 4:20 says, "The kingdom of God is not in word but in power." The power that will change people's lives is not my message. Hopefully this book will inspire you—the reader. But the power that will change lives is God's love. If there is any compelling, life-changing inspiration within the message of this book, I pray it be so only because it attests to God's power. To the Kingdom's ability to embrace you and me to wholeness and healing—fulfillment and joy. My meager words can only attest to the mighty power of God's Word and His redeeming grace.

My boyhood home in Newark, New Jersey, where I lived my first fifteen years, had an area in the basement that evoked a tantalizing fear in my boyish mind. Often today that place slips nightmarish anxiety into my dreams. The back stairwell of our three-family dwelling led to a small first-floor landing with two doors, one to the small backyard edged by the cinderblocked walls of a three-car garage, the second to the basement down a small set of stairs, under which I always felt lurked the "wild things," those monsters of the imagination. I passed storage bins, the coal bin, and the workbench where my grandfather and father worked on wood and plumbing projects, to the back wall of the basement. Behind that wall was a long, dark corridor, a black hole that tombed itself under the front stairway to the main entrance of our home on Avon Avenue. In my fifteen years of living in this home I never investigated that dark abyss. It was not until my family moved from the city of Newark that, with extension cord in hand, I took my father's work light and attached it to a beam near the entrance of this cave-like mystery, illuminating the narrow passageway. Few items were strewn on the floor. Cobwebs were suspended from the ceiling. It seemed that no one else had visited there either. Were my fears unfounded, or were they shared by others? The simple fact, I discovered, was that through the years, this place never served any purpose except to terrify me. The dark, dim unknown. It became for me what Martin Luther wrote in "A Mighty Fortress Is Our God": "And though this world, with devils filled, should threaten to undo us." In my boyhood mind, I was certain that something was living in there and that something would threaten "to undo me."

As I have grown through the years, those basement fears and horrors no longer dominate my imagination. The dark places of fear, however, have often housed in my mind, those chambers in which lurk those fears that still threaten to undo us. Some are imaginary, and over these we expend much energy for no reason at all. But some are real, created by our own sinful natures. Despite the fears, I unwisely stepped over the threshold of these dark corners of the soul.

That cavernous fear of my childhood was created by my imagination. But the dim unknowns of my adult life can still reduce me to this childish foolishness of keeping the darkened, basement cavern in the center of my mind. These dim unknowns are not figments of imagination. They are shattered fragments of wholeness marred by unwise choices:

> There is an old fable about some people who heard of a place called the "Cave of Truth." They discussed this among themselves and made further inquiries. Finally, they decided to set out in search of the cave, and after a long and difficult journey, they found it. At the entrance sat an old man, the guardian of the cave. They approached him and asked if indeed this was the Cave of Truth. He assured them that it was. They asked if they might enter. In reply, the guardian asked, "How deeply into the Cave of Truth do you want to go?" At this question, they retreated and talked among themselves. They returned and said, "We would like to enter and go just deep enough to

say we have been there." This is what I call a Marilyn Monroe faith. Asked about her beliefs, she replied, "I just believe in everything—a little bit." Truth alone is worthy of our utter devotion and ambition.[4]

I have had to ask myself the question today, which cave do I fear the most? The cave created by the tricks of the mind, recreating that dark, musty, foreboding, frightening corridor which leads to nowhere in the basement of my mind, or the Cave of Truth, in which the further I proceed, the more I will have to face uncertainty to discover a greater light, the God who stands behind the dim unknowns. Is it the cave of truth that frightens me, or is it the person to whom it will introduce me? That person being myself!

For so long, in my relationship to God and Jesus, I approached them at a protected distance, close enough to them to claim a fellowship with them, but not traveling the full distance to become one with them. I hit the "wall" at the beginning of my race through life, just after stepping over the threshold of the cave of truth. And for a while I felt emotionally exhausted before I embarked on the journey that would lead to new life.

Regarding my faith, I knew a lot about everything—"a little bit!" Not knowing the full truth about who God was and acknowledging the full truth of who I was, I lived in a shallow faith. Rooted in Him, a "little bit!" I had God's promise of new life. My choice was to live only a piece of that promise, and in that choice, I had to discover some of the greatest turmoil within my soul, a nightmare where I ran while my feet were glued stationary by immobilizing fears.

A song written by Marilyn and Alan Bergman and Michel Legrand called "Pieces of Dreams," states rather clearly the demise in which I found myself and still find myself:

Little boy lost in search of little boy found,
You go a wondering, wandering, stumbling, tumbling, round! round!
When will you find what's on the tip of your mind?
Why are you blind to all you ever were, never were, really are, nearly are?
Little boy false in search of little boy true.

Will you be ever done traveling, always unraveling you?
Running away could lead you further astray
And as for fishing in streams for pieces of dreams,
Those pieces will never fit. What is the sense of it?[5]

This contemporary, popular song reflects the New Testament parable of the prodigal son. Lost. Running. Far from home. Stumbling. Tumbling. Unable to get in touch with inner goodness and full potential. An adult, lost, searching for the person found. Seeing "nearly" what God wants me and you to become.

In my lostness and my wandering, I let my little sheep roam. The Bible refers to Jesus as "a shepherd gathering His flock." I was a little boy lost, searching for little boy found, and I scattered my flock. A wife and two small children. So many dreams flooded my life, but the discovery that I was fishing in streams for pieces of dreams, taught me that I was casting my life in places where only pieces could be caught, rather than casting my faith line in waters that would haul in a full net of promises from God. Those streams that held only pieces of dreams were far from refreshing, wooded brooks over babbling stones, placid pools, thirst-quenching springs, the sounds and feelings of which would assimilate me into the essence of nature's beauty and God's love.

I was casting my faith line into waters stagnated by that which pollutes purity, threatens natural life, and makes unattractive the natural beauty of God's creation. I began stumbling, wandering, wondering, and tumbling over the very areas in which I cast my life. Call it slime. Call it filth. I was willing to step into waters that were polluted, with bare feet, knowing that there were debris, broken glass, and ragged-edged cans guaranteed to injure me. Nevertheless, I walked into them, finding only pieces of dreams. I chose not to walk on grounds or in streams that were holy, where we are assured by God that our bare feet will not be injured nor our lives harmed.

Let me graphically make it more simple and clear. If you had the choice to drink a glass of water which has flowed from an open faucet, yellow from the rust of aged metal pipes or to cup your hands to capture the cold waters of a mountain spring, which would you choose? The question is almost too ridiculous to pose!

Yet when it comes to choices that would create a residue of impurity within our lives, we too often cast our lives in those streams that will yield only broken pieces. We do some pretty dumb things and make unwise choices.

It is God who helps us make right choices. Daniel 1:17 says, "God gave . . . knowledge and skill in all literature and wisdom; And Daniel had understanding in all visions and dreams." Leave God out of the decision process, and you will find yourself fishing in streams polluted with broken dreams. God gave you and me the greatest piece of literature from which we could learn, His Word. The Bible. We need to begin casting our lives within the Bible's ocean depths of His promise. Then we will begin comprehending how He would have us live, what choices He requires us to make, and we will turn to Him when temptations take our bare feet off of solid rock and place them on shifting sands.

Do you remember the Native American actor Iron Eyes Cody? He did the TV spot for the "Keep America Beautiful" campaign. He is seen drifting alone in a canoe, observing how our waters are being polluted. This TV commercial which shows Iron Eyes Cody with a tear running down his cheek has been broadcast for over seventeen years.

This not-so-Iron-Eyes man, whose tears convey his deep remorse for choices we make that destroy our lives, tells this story in *Guideposts*:

> Many years ago, Indian youths would go away in solitude to prepare for manhood. One such youth hiked into a beautiful valley, green with trees, bright with flowers. There he fasted. But on the third day, as he looked up at the surrounding mountains, he noticed one tall rugged peak, capped with dazzling snow. "I will test myself against that mountain," he thought. He put on his buffalo hide shirt, threw his blanket over his shoulders and set off to climb the peak.
>
> When he reached the top he stood on the rim of the world. He could see forever, and his heart swelled with pride. Then he heard a rustle at his feet, and looking down, he saw a snake. Before he could move, the snake spoke:

"I am about to die," said the snake. "It is too cold for me up here and I am freezing. There is no food and I am starving. Put me under your shirt and take me down to the valley."

"No," said the youth. "I am forewarned. I know your kind. You are a rattlesnake. If I pick you up, you will bite, and your bite will kill me."

"Not so," said the snake. "I will treat you differently. If you do this for me, you will be special. I will not harm you."

The youth resisted awhile, but this was a very persuasive snake with beautiful markings. At last the youth tucked it under his shirt and carried it down to the valley. There he laid it gently on the grass, when suddenly the snake coiled, rattled and leapt, biting him on the leg.

"But you promised—" cried the youth.

"You knew what I was when you picked me up," said the snake as it slithered away.

And now, wherever I go, I tell that story. I tell it especially to the young people of this nation who might be tempted by drugs. I want them to remember the words of the snake: "You knew what I was when you picked me up."[6]

Most of the time, we are fully aware of the ramifications of those things we "pick up," the wrong choices we make, and the effect they will have not only upon ourselves, but upon those around us. In my youth and in my adulthood, I had to suffer the damages made to self when I picked up those things which I knew were venomous when I grasped them.

My indiscretions—however sinful they were, or however innocent I was in seeking temporarily to sooth my tremendous loneliness, isolation, insecurity—never served the growth from youth to manhood. In my most recent adult years, I have waded through the shallow depths of those polluted waters as a little boy lost in search of little boy found. My choices had left me without a wife and my children without their father. From a distance today, I watch them happy and whole as a family unit, with a new husband and a stepfather—all because I picked up those "snakes," knowing how fierce their bite, but never thinking the bite would sever relationships.

I never thought of myself as a bad man. I made some bad choices, a result not only of human error but also of discerning between right and wrong and often choosing that which would not lead to "life." Careful in my attempt not to rock securely on my chair position on pity-porch, but to face myself honestly, not casting blame on anyone, I cast my life in the arms of God's grace. If I wanted to, I could dissect my life, my marriage relationship, my superficial, casual, and pseudoloyalties and find enough emotional/psychological interpretations to the weaknesses and flaws within them.

But the one I needed to deal with was the one who faced me in the mirror as I shaved on those mornings when I woke alone and isolated in my own home. My life had been filled with so many games and gamblings. I lost it all. My wife. My children. My integrity. I was completely responsible.

Now, gratefully I have cast aside some of those snakes that are always rustling at my feet, and I have begun to discover—me!

If you live your life only for yourself, you will be surrounded by many slithering temptations rustling and weaving themselves along the pathway you have chosen for yourself.

When you decide to live your life in the will of God, you will still hear those rustling sounds at your feet on the pathway He provides for your life. His path will lead to waters in which you will find, not pieces of dreams but all that He has promised—your wholeness and peace. What is rustling, then, on the pathway that He provides for you? When the world in which you live is not designed by your desires but rather designs you by God's intention of giving to you the world, His love, His life, His hope, and those waters in which you cast yourself and find glorious, fulfilling dreams?

The answer can be found in the words penned in 1901 by Maltbie D. Babcock:

> This is my Father's world, and to my listening ears
> All nature sings, and round me rings the music of the spheres.
> This is my Father's world: I rest me in the thought
> Of rocks and trees, of skies and seas;
> His hand the wonders wrought.
>
> This is my Father's world: the birds their carols raise,
> The morning light, the lily white,
> declare their Maker's praise.
> This is my Father's world: He shines in all that's fair;

In the rustling grass I hear him pass,
He speaks to me everywhere. (Italics added)

My mistakes, which maintain a powerfully strong guilt control over me, cause me often to forget one of the most powerful statements of our faith: "God is the Ruler yet!" God will not give up on you and me in this continuing battle in which snakes always slither and rustle at our feet until Jesus is fully satisfied. And that will not be until heaven and earth and you and I become one with Him.

Our unbalanced, wavering, stumbling, tumbling, wondering, and wandering footsteps in the lost pathways we have made for ourselves can turn and make a different rustling: In "the rustling grass, I can hear him pass, he speaks to me everywhere." Everywhere? Everywhere!!

Remember, this is His world. You are His child. His loving embrace surrounds you! Everywhere! And that means, even if you have picked up the snake, tucked it under your shirt, knowing full well to what that decision would lead, the rustling sounds of Jesus' feet are always there to lead you to a repentant life.

Tell Him you are tired of the snakes. Tell Him you want to hear those rustling sounds of His feet walking into your life. Not looking back with regrets, but looking to the moment in which grace, through the forgiveness of the cross, will make you and Christ one. You must stop regretting and let your life be fashioned, remolded, reshaped by forgiveness, the greatest wonder His hand will work within your life.

Do you know how much God wants to free you from your past sins and help you to learn from your gross mistakes? Jesus was not only referred to as Lord, Master, or Savior! He was also known as teacher. The disciples asked Him to "teach them to pray!" You and I can continue to ask God to teach us how to live. So many of us imprison ourselves behind those psychological and emotional fear barriers and do not know how to receive the gift of hope that God provides and promises. The Old Testament book of Micah 7:18–19 says,

> Who is a God like You,
> Pardoning iniquity

> And passing over the transgression of the remnant
>   of His heritage?
> He does not retain His anger forever, Because He
>   delights in mercy.
> He will again have compassion on us,
> And will subdue our iniquities.

Micah conveys an intentional move from anger to grace. God has not been pleased with our wrong choices or our picking up of "snakes." He gets angry with us simply because He knows what is right for us. This might seem a contradiction to the Scripture, that "God is slow to anger and abounding in love." Human beings are quick to anger. We know how to use anger, how it will move to destroy, and what will happen when it becomes the deep-seated motivating force in relationships. Slow to anger. Slow means taking a longer time than is expected or usual to act, move, go, or happen. God's anger is appropriate and necessary so that as guiding Father he leads us to where he desires us to be after all the iniquities and transgressions have been committed, and that is to grace and forgiveness. "He will again have compassion on us." He wants us to live in restoration, not to wallow in regrets. But he teaches us to learn from our regrets and our mistakes, our sins and our failures, so that we move to a restored relationship nurtured by compassion.

If God's anger assists us in understanding his unyielding and relentless desire that we grow from our mistakes, then His compassion will overshadow His anger; if, in fact, He will not even retain His anger forever, then He does not want us to live among our regrets. For if we do, we acknowledge that we do not fully understand His commitment to compassion and forgiveness, that we are controlled by our mistakes and our sins. If we are, we will never grow. Our growth comes when we see why God is angry, correct or change those things that are causing Him to be dissatisfied with us, and know that those changes and corrections are made possible by His compassion. If He never moved to compassion, we could never move to new life. This is the promise of the Incarnation. God moved compassionately into the world and sent us a Savior. Not a piece of His promise. But the promise itself.

J. Harold Ellens founder and editor in chief emeritus of the Christian Association for Psychological Studies said,

> It is the theology of grace which, if allowed to get free from the cultural and historical matrix of Scripture, is the one thing that can radically change human life.
>
> We do not begin to realize or to appreciate the radical, unconditional, and universal nature of that divine perspective until we begin to acknowledge that grace as God personally articulates it in Scripture certifies you and me as saints in the middle of our brokenness, in the process of our pathology, in spite of ourselves. There's a more striking reality even than that: grace affirms us in our pathogenesis, affirms us in the center of the process of our being sick, sinful, destructive, distorted, and in the process of creating distortion, sickness, and sin in our world. The radical option of grace is that it is precisely because of, and in the middle of, the impossibility of our sinful humanity that God *embraces* us in spite of ourselves. While we were yet sinners, Christ died for us. If grace is grace, then there is no option for me but to cast myself into the *arms* of God.[7]

Why do we then live in regrets? Why can my mind be held prisoner to those childhood caves of darkness? Why am I so reluctant to journey more deeply within that Cave of Truth, when I know that at its very center in cascading, shimmering rays of promise and hope, God's compassion and love will burst upon me? If God wants to touch us with His evident grace, compassion, forgiveness, and love, why do we not more readily touch Him and accept His free flowing grace? We grasp regrets tenaciously rather than grasp His grace more hopefully.

Mistakes. Regrets. Spending a lifetime wondering as well as knowing what went wrong along the way. I never really found me before I lost myself. My search for life began simply at the point of losing life. Had I finally become a seed that needed to fall to the ground and die? Most of my life I fished in streams for pieces of dreams. My wife indeed was a woman with promise. She had dreams for a fuller life. To my regret, I gifted her with only pieces of the dream. Shattered promises.

A particular evening replays its subtle and yet harsh visualization of what a marriage can so easily disintegrate to. My wife was at the kitchen table grading students' papers. Preoccupied with my own work and my own life, I passed the table, paused for a moment, touched her shoulders and squeezed her neck muscles to both ease her tension and caress her with care. She stopped writing, to receive the relief the brief massage brought after a hectic day at elementary school. She turned to look into my face.

Puzzlement! An aura of uncertainty radiated from her eyes rather than comfort from my touch.

"What's the matter?" I inquired.

"You touched my shoulder," she said in a tender tone of love mingled with regret that such an affectionate display from a husband was lacking.

"You touched me!"

After fifteen years of marriage, a moment of affection brought stunned acknowledgment of what had been lacking for so long. Had our lives become so busy, hectic, occupied with our own professions, our own dreams? Was there too much of a crowd in this profession of ministry where both of us were always on call and "on stage" meeting the needs of others and forgetting the yearnings and longings of each other? Had we become isolated strangers to each other in our own home, which had become merely a house in which two decent, good, loving people lived, but did not live for each other?

During one of our court-appointed family counseling sessions, my wife uttered a horrible truth to me, which will plague me long, if not the rest of my life. "This is the legal divorce, the paper divorce and decree. The first divorce occurred seven years ago!" Neither of us worked on what was apparently eroding in our lives. The waterfall of joy slowed to a trickle of long-suspended drops of what was once the essence of our relationship. Neither of us became lifestreams flowing into our common oneness as a family and as a couple. I was not flowing it to her. She could cup her hands no longer in her dream to receive the promises I once offered to her. I know I went wrong along the way; I accept the majority of the blame, an acknowledgment that I might avoid making in our society, which affirms that it always "takes two." My indiscretions shattered any hope of a redemptive quality in our home. And so, her wedding band was slipped off and gently placed on the kitchen windowsill, with a glimmering of the sun's rays upon the gold band, all that was left of our lives. Reflections.

Regrets and mistakes are the bars of the prison I have made for myself, in which my cellmates are dragons and fears. Though I was afraid to enter the cellar dungeon in my boyhood home, I wound up living there as a man.

Within that darkness I did meet someone, One who gives me hopes to live for rather than regrets and mistakes to live by.

Is there hope when all has been reduced to doom? Can the shattered pieces of promises become whole promises of life again? Can I look into God's eyes and willingly and honestly explain to Him my sins? Offer to Him my sins? Is there a tomorrow, a new dawning after the storm's desolation? Because there is a God, there is also an answer. Yes!

Regrets. Mistakes. Dragons. God calls us beyond these fears. Ranier Maria Rilke in his "Letter to a Young Poet," speaks to me, a young writer, who is just rekindling dreams, reordering his life, and allowing God to restore his dreams:

> How should we be able to forget those ancient
> myths that are at the beginning of all peoples,
> the myths about dragons that at the last moment
> turn into princesses;
> perhaps all the dragons of our lives are princesses
> who are only waiting to see us once beautiful and brave.
> Perhaps everything terrible is in its deepest being
> something helpless that wants help from us.
> So you must not be frightened, if a sadness rises up
> before you larger than any you have ever seen;
> if a restiveness, like light and cloud-shadows
> passes over your hands and over all you do.
> You must think that something is happening with you,
> that life has not forgotten you,
> that it holds you in its hand;
> it will not let you fall. . . .[8]

Something helpless in my life wanted help from me. This helplessness called me to become more desirous of following God's will, asking His forgiveness. God was waiting within me to see me once more beautiful and brave. He wants you strong and whole also. Whatever the sadness or loss in your life, there is the full promise of God, the strength of His loving embrace. Jesus has not forgotten you. He holds you in His hand. He will not let you fall from His embrace.

How is one's hope regained? How do we move beyond regrets and mistakes to seasons of new life? We can continue living, not in regret, cursing our fate, despising our own lives. But we can remember the Love of God. We can learn to become happy and content. The Lord teaches us about life through lessons learned. We can learn to like *us!*

God's Loving Embrace is about an embrace that gathers to itself pieces of broken promises. We can turn to see Him, the one who touches our shoulder with His caressing care, stunning us in the evident pressure of His touch.

God's grace and compassion will move you to a new level of living. I am humbled by the promises it provides to me today. No longer need we live in broken dreams. We can become what Henry David Thoreau described:

> To him whose elastic and vigorous thought keeps
> pace with the sun, the day is a perpetual morning.
> It matters not what the clocks say or the attitudes
>   and labor of men.
> Morning is when . . . . there is dawn in me.

God's loving embrace gently awakens you to the morning. And morning is when there is dawn in you.

When my marriage ended and when my daughters sat on the knee of another man's security and love, I was in grief and deep mourning that knew no dawn. Yet my life to the present has served one purpose: to live in the moment, fishing in the stream for peaceful dreams.

If there is a new dawn in me and you, the truth is that there is tomorrow. God's embrace leads us there, and if need be, carries us there.

Be still and hear the tender rustling on your path. It is the feet of Jesus Christ the Savior. He wants to pick you up, to place you under the arms of His embrace. When you let Him lift you to His embrace, you will know who He is. In "your heart of hearts" you will know Him as your Hope and Comfort.

Feel His evident touch. Your life can be radiant again. For did He not say He was the shepherd who leads us into green pastures? He wants us to take our broken, shattered, pieces-of-promises lives into that Cave of Truth, all the way in to discover the truth of His love and forgiveness, to feel His evident touch in green pastures of hope and faith.

CHAPTER 3

God's Evident Touch

When God shared with us the brilliant colors of the rainbow as His promise of new life, it was His way of telling us that life is far from bland. It is excitingly vibrant and spectacularly reflective of His creative touch in every facet of life.

His touch makes you beautiful. As part of His exquisite creation we know that our lives experience the change of seasons. Every season has its own charm, beauty, hue, and flavor. We also go through dry spells. Our emotions can become brittle.

Then there are days when rays of hope are interspersed among the cluttered, dry, crisp weeds. Even the frosty winds suddenly surge with a tropic warmth through life's heavy overcast.

The poet Shelley said, "If winter comes, can spring be far behind?" As God touches you, there is always the promise of new life. The Song of Solomon fascinates us with its account of this creative process and evident design in life's changes.

> For, lo, the winter is past,
> The rain is over *and* gone.
> The flowers appear on the earth;
> The time of singing has come,
> And the voice of the turtledove

Is heard in our land.
The fig tree puts forth her green figs,
And the vines *with* the tender grapes
Give a good smell.[1]

There is always a glimpse of dawn, even through life's darkest problems. Life is never completely black or bleak. Because God lives within you, you are not destitute of light. For we are not without hope. A surface perfectly black cannot reflect light.

But not one human child of God is perfectly black. God touches your life with light and promise. If you look deeply within your life, you will find a light that flickers with hope.

God's hand is evident within all of creation. It creates a marvelous picture of lives displaying His splendor and glory. I knew that His hand was always touching my life, designing me according to His will. But I never imagined this creative hand would lead me into one of the darkest moments of my life.

"For many years, God's hand has been very evident in the direction of my life."

These words were spoken by a nervous, jittery, inexperienced teenager to the anticipation of expectant eyes and ears of a proud congregation listening to their youth express statements of faith. Burke White, my minister and mentor, had chosen me to be one of the six senior high students to participate in this special youth Sunday.

As a young boy, I felt the powerful presence of God's evident hand persistently guiding me down a path that would lead to full-time Christian service.

It was this evident, guiding hand that twenty-three years later directed my life to the Collegiate Church of New York City, America's oldest congregation and our country's first corporation.

In the fall of 1981 Dr. Norman Vincent Peale invited me to become one of the Collegiate ministers of this historic Reformed Church in America. I was installed as the forty-eighth minister in line of succession since 1628. It was a tremendous affirmation to be selected by one of the century's most renowned proclaimers of the faith.

God's evident hand was definitely influencing the direction of my career and ministry. By all indications my ministry was reflecting an early level of success, an intense and steady escalation, which today remains a complete surprise to me, an acknowledged gift and leading of God. Life was bright with God's promises for an exciting career.

Seneca said,

> If any one gave you a few acres, you would say that you had received a benefit; can you deny that the boundless extent of the earth is a benefit? . . . Whence comes the breath which you draw; the light by which you perform the actions of your life? The blood by which your life is maintained? The meat by which your hunger is appeased? The true God has planted, not a few oxen, but all the herds on their pastures throughout the world, and furnished food to all the flocks; he has ordained the alternation of summer and winter . . . he has invented so many arts and varieties of voice, so many notes to make music. We have implanted in us the seeds of all ages, of all arts; and God our Master brings forth our intellects from obscurity.[2]

God placed me in Manhattan, a boundless city, with the myriad colors of diversity, rich in beauty, a beauty often obscured by society's intense problems. For many, life is bleak here. The city is filled with hurting people, dramatized by the multidimensional, varied ethnic flavor of lifestyles, needs, and hurts.

In coming to New York, I was able to say, like Seneca, "If anyone gave you a few acres, you would say that you received a benefit." To minister in New York, one of the world's greatest cosmopolitan thoroughfares, has been a great benefit and blessing. Such a call by the Collegiate Church and Norman Vincent Peale was certainly bringing my life and ministry "from obscurity."

It was in this same setting, in which I was called to love and serve people, that the discovery of my own hurt and confusion would emerge. Soon I would discover that my own problems could no longer be obscured. I had to deal with them.

This was a metropolis filled with chaos and confusion, where people often do not see the sky and seldom touch the earth as they drift aimlessly through the canyon of city streets. I would soon be shocked to learn that I was one of them.

As the fringes of my own life were beginning to fray, it was difficult to perceive that this guiding, evident hand of God was the motivating force behind the trauma which would begin the refining process of my own life.

At the height of apparent success and security in ministry, the struggle began to intensify. Life was becoming bleak and black for me. Crystalizing around me was a frozen, emotional wasteland.

At age fifteen the message of faith I proclaimed was one of the guiding, evident hand of God in our lives. There has been no deviation from this truth through the years, except to shift slightly in its emphasis. It is more than God's hand that is evident in life today. It is His loving embrace, an embrace that sees us through the most difficult experiences of life.

God's hand has always been discernible in my life. It has been strong and encouraging, unfathomable in its ability to direct and gently guide.

But then it happened. This same gentle hand was to lead me into the deep pain of the valley. In the journey the need for those hands to become a life support and a healing loving embrace increased.

At the height of my emotional trauma, I saw God's hands as being more than merely evident. They would lift and embrace a hurting individual with warmth that would seek after his soul, awake the spirit within, and provide a hope and joy when life around him and within began to collapse.

In *Zorba the Greek,* Nikos Kazantzakis makes a statement regarding our trust in God when we are thrust upon the jagged mountain edges of life, precariously holding on to our last thread of hope. It has to do with our attitude about facing life's problems:

> The idea's everything. Have you faith? Then a splinter from an old door becomes a sacred relic. Have you no faith? Then the whole Holy Cross itself becomes an old doorpost to you.[3]

The attitude with which you face your problem will determine how the problem either strengthens you with the potential for growth or defeats you in the wake of its adversity. If you have faith in God's loving embrace, your problem will take on the design of God's creative reformation and revelation within you.

You will see the loving, redemptive power of the cross in everything that is happening to you. Even your problem will deepen the brilliance of the colorful fabric of your life, for woven into your life is the intentional design of God's will. It is difficult to comprehend, but the painful experiences might just be the result of God having us right where He wants us at this moment in our lives so that we might depend upon Him more.

> Fear not, I am with Thee; O be not dismayed,
> For I am thy God, and will still give thee aid;
> I'll strengthen thee, help thee, and cause thee to stand,
> Upheld by my righteous, omnipotent hand.

> When through fiery trials thy pathways shall lie,
> My grace, all-sufficient, shall be thy supply;
> The flame shall not hurt thee; I only design
> Thy dross to consume, and thy gold to refine.

There it is! This great idea that is everything. God's loving embrace is always with you, to strengthen you, uphold you, bless you, redesign you. He prevents you from falling into the great abyss of life's uncertainties.

We are fragile creatures yet have the opportunity to call on God to give us strength for living. The valley and wilderness are never barren of God's presence. Kazantzakis says it is more than just attitude, however. It comes down to choosing God as the source of life, to reaching out to grasp His hand:

> Zorba, we are little grubs, minute grubs on the small leaf of a tremendous tree. This small leaf is the earth. The other leaves are the stars that you see moving at night. We make our way on this little leaf examining it anxiously and carefully. . . . Some men, the more intrepid ones, reach the edge of the leaf. From there we stretch out, gazing into chaos. We tremble. We guess what a frightening abyss lies beneath us. . . . Bent thus over the awe-inspiring abyss, with all our bodies and all our souls we tremble with terror. From that moment begins the great

change. Some grow dizzy and delirious, others are afraid; they try to find an answer to strengthen their hearts and they say: God! Others again, from the edge of the leaf, look over the precipice calmly and bravely and say: I like it.[4]

There are times when we cannot look calmly and bravely over the precipice of life. We do not like what we see. We are frightened. Our lives collapse in shambles. We do not live as rightly as we should. To like ourselves is often a difficult assignment. We despair over what we have done to others or to ourselves. We fret over our own sinfulness.

Yes, many times in life our walk is filled with fear, especially when we drift aimlessly on this suspended leaf of life. Peering over the edge of life, we tremble, trying to find an answer to strengthen our hearts. And the answer that sustains us always is: *God!*

He is always there: "Fear not, I am with thee." He is on that leaf or underneath you to support you when you fail and fall. In such an embrace you discover that you never drift aimlessly because the one in whom we live and move and have our being is always present. We can lean upon Him and let Him lift us.

It was when I was broken, wounded, abandoned, and desolate that I discovered the real faith that God provides. It was necessary however, in looking over the edge of the jagged cliff, the jagged edges of my life, that I call on His name and rely on Him for a love that would see me through.

I was discovering that God is faithful to His promises, fulfilling my life when all seemed empty and critically dim. I was yearning for the radiance that I saw on Martin Aquaah's face as his life was emersed in the love of God.

Jesus said, "If I be lifted up, drawing all people unto myself, I will release within them the gift of life."

He said this to imply the manner by which He would die. He was lifted up for you. Drawing you to Himself. Bringing your life into His. What a marvelous, loving embrace. No other embrace can compare to its steadfast intensity. It conveys to us the Lord's willingness and His ability to assist us in overcoming any adversity, awakening our dark lives to a new dawn.

Such a love seems incomprehensible when life splinters

and our self-esteem is shattered. Then we always see through the mirrors of our experiences dimly. The dense fog of uncertainty mystifyingly surrounds us. Yet penetrating through it is the loving embrace of God, which allows us to see more clearly the path through the valley of shadows.

The paradox of my life at this point in my career, and more importantly in my spiritual quest, is that while I affirm the loving grace and embrace of God in my capacity as minister, my people are discovering a minister, one of their equals when his persona, his "mask" is removed.

Frightened.
Longing.
Searching.
Struggling.
Hoping.

For the embrace of a friend to love and comfort him. For hands that are warm and strong in their greeting, hands, not extended to keep one at arm's length, but extended to keep one within arm's reach.

In this book, you will discover that ministers quest after the same dreams in life, the need-fulfilling experiences for which their own people struggle. Ministers deal with the same hurts. They stand before their people as human beings, who have skinned their knees after being tripped up by life's problems and by wrong choices. They can also be lifted up by the unexpected, surprising embrace of a God who promises that He will lift us and release within us the gift of new life.

Jesus is a lover of our souls, broken though they may be. His hands lift us, and His love remolds us because it is His good pleasure and desire that He renew and restore us and make us whole. The process may be a painful one. But we are comforted by God's loving embrace—His most evident touch.

CHAPTER 4

The Embrace That Binds

I discovered the binding love of God the day I was forced to face the severing of the bond of love in my home.

Looking into my eyes as she leaned over the kitchen stove, her face reflecting the light from the exhaust hood over the range and her mind musing over the emotional pain of the news she was about to break, my wife uttered the words that would change the course of my life, words that plunged me into horror and panic.

"I want you to set me free!!!"

With disbelief and numbness I clearly focused the word in my mind.

Divorce!

Not a trial separation. My wife made the firm decision that she no longer wanted to be married—to me. Rejection! An important person in my life was rejecting me. No one in my life had ever seen me as disposable before.

Again, the frightening word centered itself in my mind. Divorce! *Divorce!*

I never thought it would happen to me. To us. To my family. In one quick, unexpected announcement, the world crumbled beneath my feet. The thought of losing my family was unbearable. Swept into the undertow of my wife's decision to leave me was my own self-esteem.

Was I worthless to someone else? Fifteen years of marriage! Was there no reason to preserve it or at least seek counseling to help us solve our problems?

After I processed this horrifying information through my mind and mustered the little composure I had left, I was again gripped by fear when I thought of the damage this situation could do to the credibility of my ministry. Even my professional well-being was now threatened.

Laurie, our oldest daughter was already surrounded by the American divorce phenomenon with her peer group in school. She saw firsthand much of the hurt and fear of her personal friends, and she had even asked us, "Mommy and Dad, will you ever get divorced?"

My wife assured our daughter, "Laurie, Daddy and I would never get divorced. We love each other."

On this evening, however, Laurie disintegrated into sobs of fear. The threat to her family she feared the most was confirmed by her mother, who told this frightened child that Mommy and Daddy were no longer going to live together. She did not love me.

In an instant, the dreams she had for tomorrow, were overshadowed by doubts created by an adult world. Her home was collapsing. She was now fully suspicious of the dependability of that adult world, of the integrity of her parent's word. We had lied to her! For this we shall always bear the responsibility.

There were many problems within our marriage. Stressful situations, attitudes, and circumstances ate away at the very foundation of our home with acidic potency.

One of our heavy burdens through the years was that we were always viewed as the "perfect couple." The expectation level of those who viewed our lives from the outside often made it difficult to allow ourselves to live a real and normal life. And when I, especially, fell short of that expectation level, I found myself riddled with guilt.

We were also a good-looking couple. My wife was often likened to Natalie Wood or Linda Carter and I was urged in jest (and seriously by some) to pursue a career in soaps or modeling.

These comments stated to us how the world viewed us by appearances. But the world, family, and friends, really did not know what was tormenting us internally and what we were struggling with personally.

Beneath the veneer of our attractiveness was a layer of confusion and no real identity. I was uncertain of my personal identity. Who I appeared to be on the outside was far different from the identity I was struggling with inside. The same was true for my wife. What we appeared to be was not who we really knew ourselves to be. And neither my wife nor I helped each other to discover who we really were. We completely ignored it, and therefore our relationship starved itself. The request for a divorce came without any desire to remedy the malady of our marriage. We had coexisted but had no relationship based on commitment and intimacy. We did not know each other's soul.

Our love and companionship were taken for granted. Complacency overshadowed the need to work diligently on some of our problems. Had we given energy to resolving these tensions we could have nurtured our marriage, remolded our relationship, created a more sound love, and worked on improving our cancerous weaknesses. We simply did not address them, at least not openly to each other. Quietly, the relationship was being terminated.

Without a doubt, I loved this woman to whom I had been married for fifteen years. My problem was I did not know how to show it. My wife was starved for my affection. Assuming that she knew I loved her, I demonstrated my love only superficially.

We traveled on parallel tracks, sufficiently satisfied to see the joining of our two lives at the perspective point. But as we lived out our relationship, we never seemed to be joined together. There was no common embrace of love. We were adults playing house.

One day my wife decided to take a different path. The road would not include me.

Months of therapy had given me the opportunity to ascertain who I was, to discover a man I never thought existed. I was beginning to love and accept myself, sorting out those areas of my life which were preventing me from being a whole person. While this supportive base of therapy bolstered my desire to heal our relationship, strengthen it, and perhaps discover each other for the first time, my wife's brief encounter with counseling seemed to give her the courage and impetus to begin the process of divorce.

Her anger was unleashed and knew no control. She took the bold position of confidence in her decision to terminate fifteen valuable years of a relationship between two people who genuinely cared for each other.

Our home had moved into the valley of dry bones. We were trying to plant roots in rather inhospitable rocks, reaching and striving for rare moments of sunshine. Living in our home was like climbing hand over hand up different slopes. At times it was like living in low lying, barren wastelands, with waterbeds and streams almost completely dry. Underfoot beds of fallen, brittle leaves had gathered.

Both of us had been struggling to discover a fresh beauty in our marriage. I was making radical readjustments. I needed to change to give our relationship integrity and strength. My own personhood and self-esteem, if they were to survive, required that I change—totally!

My commitment to healing myself and our marriage was based on my love for my wife and family. I was determined to return to this family as a whole person, renewed and fully re-committed. My determination was based on the fact and faith that all problems are reconcilable and solvable, if faith and God are allowed to remold people. And if two people willingly commit themselves to this effort.

A week before my wife asked me for a divorce, I remember standing in the kitchen with her just after she finished the evening dishes. I turned her around toward me. Crying, I said, "I'm working on a lot. It's going to take some time. But I just want you to know I love you!" I remember the nervous look on her face now, a look that I later discovered came from her knowledge that she would be soon asking me for a dissolution of our marriage.

In all my counseling sessions with couples I had seen that couples whose relationships seemed hopeless could grow to understand each other if they still had the foundation of a genuine love for each other. The commitment to that love helped them to restore integrity to their lives and love.

My redemptive and reconciling faith had convinced me that God could breathe life again even into the dry bones of our existence—if we were willing to place our marriage in His hands. The two of us could not commit ourselves to this effort. Both of us must forever deal with our unwillingness to dialogue and work through our problems.

And so a new and closer relationship began for me that day. Though I didn't recognize it at the time, I was swept up in the loving embrace of God.

Despite all the anger, which has now been resolved, the hate, that was eating away at my integrity and my ability to love, the resentment which underlay my every action, it is still my prayer that this woman with whom I shared fifteen years of married life and had two children knows that loving embrace of God for herself, that she discovers a new life, radiantly resplendent with God's promises. Despite all my pain, I am able to say she was one of the greatest gifts God ever gave to me.

My wife's request for a divorce, strange though it may sound, was also a gift that set me free to begin the inward journey that would lead to the discovery, not of a new man within me, but of a more complete and whole human being. A man fulfilled in the loving embrace of God.

Every facet of my personhood has either been explored or is still being uncovered.

There would be no smooth transition in this divorce. Many would be hurt by our inability to work through our problems. My major concern was that my daughters were fully secure in my love for them as a father. After all, I was the one leaving the home, vacating the house, throwing an empty void into their lives.

Laurie's child psychologist, who assisted us initially with some of our marriage problems, asked me to explain to my daughter why her mommy and daddy could no longer live together. This request denied me the responsibility, privilege, and opportunity of speaking lovingly and compassionately with my daughter. To suggest that Mommy and Daddy could no longer live together, in this counseling session seemed clinical and devoid of intimate feelings which otherwise could have been shared only between a father and his daughter.

I was outraged!

To convey something so devastating and hopeless at this time was inappropriate. This therapist denied me the opportunity to initiate this conversation with my daughter in my own tender, loving way. Her professional style denied me the private moment of talking heart to heart, through tears and hugs, with my little girl.

Emotionally, I was still making every effort to redirect the collision course of our marriage. I still saw little rays of hope. The therapist clipped that thread and denied me the opportunity to share emotions with my daughter. The encounter was completely sterilized of compassion and love.

The statements were cold, calculated, and intentional. I watched the twinkling constellation of stars in my daughter's eyes drown in a flood of tears. Hope dwindled before my eyes.

In the days that followed self-preservation thrust each of us into a barrage of innuendos and insults. Our expressions of rage were filled with harsh honesty. Unleashed upon me were years of anger and resentment, many accusations that I was hearing for the first time. Feelings disguised through the years by a simple unwillingness to communicate. Some were justified. Some were used only to justify a spouse's decision to terminate a marriage. Both of us stood accused by the other's resentments.

It suddenly became clear to me. Before me was a woman I really did not know. And I was a man unknown by my wife. Rather than resolving any differences, she told me that she had no feelings of love left for me. I was tossed to the wind with the withered leaves beginning to collect at my feet. And like one of those leaves I was brittle and crushed.

Each approach to my wife resulted in cuts, bruises, and lacerations that tore my emotions wide open. All we seemed able to do was intentionally hurt each other.

In my emotional pain that evening, I went to my daughters' bedrooms, starting first with Laurie.

I lifted her from a sound sleep. Sweeping the covers off

of her comfortably secured body, I cradled her in my arms, sobbing, asking her for forgiveness for being the uncaring father her mother accused me of being.

Unrestrained I clung to Laurie, my firstborn child. Gently, she stroked the back of my head, giving me comfort and security. I sobbed uncontrollably.

Here was an eleven-year-old offering solace to a broken father. Besides God's loving embrace, there was this loving embrace between a father and his daughter in the darkest moment of their lives. It was the strongest, tenderest embrace I ever felt in my own home. It will be a treasured gift always.

Picking myself up off the floor, I made my way to Sarah's room. She slept so peacefully in her pink and blue comforter. The lace-trimmed curtains hung crisply starched in gracefulness, reminding me of the precious little life I was about to cradle in my arms.

Looking down upon her, I recalled how we almost lost Sarah at birth. She weighed less than five pounds. I watched in fear as doctors tried to sustain her life when respiratory complications set in and her lungs collapsed. Her life was maintained by a life-support system in a special neonatal center. The scars on her chest, where tubes were inserted to inflate the lungs, to this day, serve to remind me that she was a miracle baby for us. And now I saw a new scar being developed in her life, from the breach of her family.

Again I cried as I held Sarah, feeling her as an extension of my personal identity. The wrenching separation from these two precious children, my daughters, seemed more than I could endure.

When Sarah was born, I assisted the doctor in her delivery. Inspired by the miracle of birth, I thrilled over the opportunity to cut her umbilical cord. With one snip, she was separated from her mother's womb, becoming an independent bundle of God's miraculous love.

Now I was cutting another cord. The family tie, the cord holding us together was being snipped by two parents who were too arrogant and proud to work out their difficulties.

I prayed that Sarah would be able to handle this crisis with strength, just as she had survived her first hours of life.

This became my daily prayer for her, and I have seen that God is answering that prayer.

As my family relationship was severed, God's loving embrace became ever more clear and necessary for me. Strangely, I even felt a new closeness to the children.

As I returned them to the security of their comfortable beds, I affirmed my faith that nothing could separate us from the love of God, nor from the love of our relationship. Not even divorce!

As long as our lives were placed in God's tender keeping, nothing could sever us from His love.

Divorce would even bring us closer, cementing our love. The journey through the valley can bring us closer to God.

I was not only peering over the edge of the leaf of life into the dismal abyss which was referred to in *Zorba The Greek*. I was falling into the frightening unknown. In the privacy of our bedroom, in emotional collapse, I felt my body gyrate in spasms. I was completely distraught, crushed, abandoned, and out of control.

Yet as long as Christ was in the abyss, it would be a journey *through* the shadow of death: "In the beginning was the Word, and the Word was with God, and the Word was God. In Him was life, and the life was the light of men. And the light shines in the darkness."[1] Each time you affirm this thought, you can claim that God will lead you through the valley into life that is brilliant with joy.

My wife and I mutually agreed that I would be the one to leave the house. She taught school only two blocks away, and Laurie attended the same school. It was easier for me to relocate than to stubbornly insist that I remain and they leave. My wife was the one who wanted the divorce, and I could have been hardnosed and claimed my home. After all, my church owned the house.

While each accusation inflicted new wounds on one who was already devastated, each accusation, each vindictive remark also resulted in a more complete reliance on God's loving embrace and grace to sustain me. The more difficult life became, the more reliant I became on God to uphold me. The more hurtful the situation, the more binding God's loving embrace became.

Letters from my wife soon evoked more fear and anxiety. I dreaded going to the mailbox. Days would go by before I collected the accumulated mail. But the day she wrote that she had changed the locks on our doors I was enraged. That day, after moving beyond my rage, I found myself at a positive turning point.

The barrier set up by my wife opened up a new door of trust and reliance on God. In turning to Him, I closed the door to a fifteen-year chapter of my life. I took the step to begin struggling on my own and with Him.

I was now completely and symbolically alone. I was homeless. Even though I moved in with my parents, my identity as man, husband, father, and provider vanished.

Determined not to let anger govern me, I prayed, "Oh God, search me, and know me, and if you find any anger in my heart, lead me unto eternal life."

Complete loneliness! Thirty-eight years old and isolated! Desolated! Rejected for the first time. Tossed to the wind, struggling to see, once again, God's evident hand in my life. My marriage had been crumbling for a long time, but it was not the only aspect of my life that was crumbling. I had failed. And failed miserably.

My personal difficulties riddled me with anxiety. My finances fell into a shambles. Bank overdraft notices began to appear, and a few of my major credit cards were canceled, both indicating that life was in a state of disarray.

Before I moved out of the house, our sexual relationship was incompatible, practically nonexistent. I fell to a critical state of despair when I increased an intake of Sominex pills from two to eleven at one time to get to sleep, to stay asleep, and to escape life's problems.

I left notes on the kitchen counter about my desperation and the thoughts of my own precarious life. Reaching out for help, I never realized that fear was immobilizing my wife. What was most painful was the discovery that when I was hurting the most, the place from which I thought support, comfort, hope, and encouragement would come, left me. How selfish of me, the person from whom she sought support, comfort, hope, and encouragement, to withdraw emotionally from her. Our relationship was bankrupt for years.

But I was left with something powerful to sustain me. It was more than God's evident hand in my life. It was God's loving embrace, the embrace that would bind me more closely to Him.

Nothing troubled me more in my separation and divorce proceedings than the personal indictments which were made against us as a couple. These accusations reflected upon us not only as a married couple but as a clergy couple. In my attempt to be honest in the writing of this book, I admit that I point a finger directly at myself to show my inner weakness which contributed to the weakness of my marriage. I had dedicated my life to God yet totally neglected the meditative and spiritual disciplines that would have strengthened my life.

In our moment of crisis, when I grasped onto the Scriptures for their powerful ability to offer renewal, reconciliation, and forgiveness, I found myself in faith's greatest turmoil. The letters to the Corinthians taught me that love keeps no record of wrongs. Yet in our moment of desperation my wife made a judgment about my faith that stunned me into an awareness that any effort to reconcile was futile. She had no desire to talk about forgiveness.

My use of a simple Scripture, "I can do all things through Christ who strengthens me," was greeted with the response, "Ron, you've always hidden behind your religion!"

I was stunned!

This statement, directed at the very root of my nature as a person of faith, forced me to grapple with two thoughts.

Was her interpretation correct?

Were we incompatible not only as a couple, but also in our spiritual lives?

Perhaps we had no wholeness in our marriage because we were not in harmony with the Spirit. Unless we relied on God to heal us, there would be no possibility for love to do its redeeming work. We could not agree on the role of our faith in healing us. Not only were we tossing our marriage away. Our faith was being cast aside with it.

Not only was I feeling abandoned, but my faith was faltering. To have my faith and soul pierced, my belief system held suspect, was the most tormenting aspect of the demise of my marriage.

My wife, after fifteen years in shared ministry, was now accusing me of hiding behind my faith. Did she hate me this much? Was her rage against me that violent? Finally, I had to admit that many of her feelings were justified.

Inherent in this accusation I sensed the personal denial that God could forgive us of our faults and our sins, a promise made by Him if we were willing to turn our lives and our marriage over to Him. I was willing.

"You have always hidden behind your religion" played havoc with my mind. It tormented me into sleepless nights (and a heavier reliance on Sominex). Yet the accusation immersed me even more deeply in my faith. All I could think of was the verse from the hymn,

> "Guide me, O thou great Jehovah,
> Pilgrim through this barren land."

My life, at this moment was a barren wilderness. I did not seek to hide behind my religion. I sought comfort in being led by God.

Psalm 27:5 says,

> For in the time of trouble
> He shall hide me in his pavilion.

This crisis directed me more intentionally into the depths of my faith. It was the only place I knew where to turn.

On our last night together in our home, we bared the result of intentional choices not to turn, together, to God.

Embarrassingly, I share those indictments here to acknowledge this to be the truth for many people, Christians, unbelievers, and clergy. We often turn away from the first place from which we should seek guidance and help. We turn away from God.

Had we been a couple daily disciplined in the reading of the Bible, we would have been equipped through the years with the resource to sustain our marriage through life's adversities. Had *I* been more deeply immersed in the faith I proclaimed to others, I would have been a more honest man to her and to my congregation. I was not hiding in my faith, but certainly I began discerning ways I had used faith to cover up my weaknesses. Faith had become a safe and reclusive arena in which I could give the illusion that all was well with my world.

Paul said, "With Christ in you, you have the power to overcome all adversity!" Now I was wondering how much Christ was really living within me.

We were a clergy couple, but we rarely opened the pages of the Bible for devotional time together. Such sharing would have held our relationship in the embracing love of God, deepening our lives in love as the fruit of God's blessing.

Let me be more emphatically honest.

Rarely opened the Bible??

We *never* opened the Bible!

Study provided me with hours to be immersed in the Word. The Bible was my source of sermon inspiration, of insight into inspiring messages for a congregation gathered to hear these words of hope, of insight on how to be loving. We never studied it for these guidelines.

As far as reading the Bible for personal strength, for everyday living, as part of our devotional life, we never cracked the pages of the Bible. And our marriage was as brittle as our Bible's binding.

There was an invisible dust on the devotional aspect of our married life.

The Bible provided us with an illusion of a couple centered in the Word. The invisible dust on it revealed lives that were withering. Our marriage began accumulating the cobwebs of the misuse of the greatest power for living, God's Holy Word. Without devotion to it, we made wrong choices throughout our marriage. The final one was to terminate the marriage.

Misusing God's Holy Word. In our darkest hour, when our marriage dissipated, we could not look together into the Bible for the light we needed to illuminate our darkened path.

My marriage and my ministry were branded with the indictment that we lived the facade of faith. My heart was burdened with this incrimination.

Then I turned to prayer. "Let's pray about this problem. Let's get on our knees, this moment, in this room, in the privacy of our lives with God, and turn this pathetic state of affairs over to Him," I cried.

She shook her head slightly: "No!" The second indictment was leveled at me. As a couple, as two people who had given their lives to the ministry, we were unwilling and unable to get on our knees and surrender ourselves to God.

My mind was now in a total quandary. For years I had led congregations in prayer. At every meeting the minister was expected to provide the spiritual tone. Offer the prayer. Those who felt unqualified, afraid to pray, or unwilling did not have to as long as the minister was there.

During family gatherings Ron Cadmus was always asked to bless the meal: "The minister is here. He'll lead us in prayer."

My father-in-law used to joke, "Now we'll get a real prayer." At a function for my wife's family, her aunt rather crudely insulted my sincerity by saying, "Well, he knows how to offer good prayers. It's his job!" Professionalism, in her eyes, lessened the integrity of my prayers.

Always the minister had to pray. And often I was so spiritually starved. I wanted others to offer words of faith and lift me to a closer relationship with God. Prayer was merely routine. My wife never prayed for me orally. But then neither did I for her.

At the dinner table, brief prayers were always the result of passing the buck of responsibility. How easy it was to ask the children to pray. But while we were trying to nurture them in the ways of faith and prayer, we were also escaping the responsibility.

Without prayer, our relationship was powerless. Our marriage was stretched until it collapsed.

Fifteen years married as a clergy couple, as a young Christian man and woman, and our life lacked the very elements that would have prevented us from becoming stagnant in our marriage or dishonest in our feelings and behavior.

We never read the Bible.

Our heads were never bowed in prayer.

A saying claims, "Seven days without prayer, makes one *weak!*" We had fifteen years, 5,675 days, without prayer. We were deficient in strength that comes from the Word of God, from the power of prayer.

Consequently, as a couple, as a clergy couple, we lacked the ruling power or authority of God, and a pathetic scene unfolded in our home. Our relationship was feeble, infirm, debilitated, invalid, sickly. Our individual lives were just as pale and sickly.

As a couple, we were emotionally, physically, and spiritually broken. Our marriage was over. Surprisingly, I went to bed with my wife that last night for the first time in many months.

The moon's rays shone through our bedroom window silhouetting us in the darkness of our lives, casting a sullen image on us both.

Rising within me was a passionate yearning to make love to her one last time, to restore and savor the feeling of who we were when our love was at its best. This feeling remained a silent dream as I listened to her subdued sobs.

Determined not to leave the darkness of this evening without a sense of resolve and determined not to let hatred eat away my respect, caring, and, yes, even love for this woman, I reached for her hand in tenderness.

"I don't care what you say or how you feel about what I am going to do. Forget that I am your husband. I don't fill that capacity anymore."

I took her hand and began to pray, for us, for our peace, for our forgiveness, so that the pounding pains of anxiety within each of us could subside.

"Lord, forgive me for all that I have done that wronged this woman." She uttered back through her tears, "Forgive me too."

When we were married on August 14, 1971, the minister preached on Ephesians 4:32, the verse the two of us had selected as the foundation of our marriage: "Be kind to one another, tenderhearted, forgiving one another, just as God in Christ also forgave you."

Ironically this verse had no real power for us during the critical crisis in our life because we failed to allow it to speak to us.

Look at the verse more closely: "Be kind to one another, tenderhearted, forgiving one another."

Forgiving one another. Yes, we often did this in our relationship, but we did not live the text to its full intention. We were able to forgive only to the extent of our human ability.

How often we say we forgive someone when in reality we harbor grudges through the years, never relinquishing the offense against us or forgiving the offender. A bitter thought about someone or some situation is never completely released. We are held captive to past grievances against people even long after they have died.

Seeing someone who has offended us can call to memory so many harsh thoughts and bad experiences. Human nature does not allow us to forgive fully and Paul knew this. That is why he goes one step beyond human ability to forgive when he says, "forgiving one another *just as* Jesus Christ has forgiven you" (italics added).

The difference is in following the example of the Savior, fashioning our lives in His likeness. We cannot forgive. Only Christ can forgive through us.

The problem in our marriage? We could not be *just as* Jesus was, nor were we willing to allow Him the opportunity to work His forgiveness in us.

As this was the prayer for our relationship when we were united in marriage, I wanted this to be my prayer the last night I was to lie near my wife.

I left her, not with a kiss on her lips, but with a prayer from my lips to her heart, spoken from the fullness of my love for her. It was my hope that prayer would be the gentle, loving, sustaining embrace for our survival and growth through and beyond this ordeal.

It was the first real prayer we ever shared.

It was also the last.

I awakened the following morning to a new dawn. My life had been emptied of strength. A decision was made in my heart that morning! Before I took that first step into my life as a man alone, I was going to make the step, not alone.

In walking out of my home, after hugging my eldest daughter, I was going to walk into the loving embrace of God.

Those arms always assure forgiveness. In that embrace one could discover the grace that provides hope. Through that touch, there would be the assurance of healing. I had made many mistakes in this marriage. With God's help, I was going to turn those mistakes into lessons.

Divorce was creating an unfathomable distance from one I had loved for fifteen years. But this same divorce was creating an unfathomable closeness to a God, who did love me unconditionally and who forgave my sins through His Son's loving embrace.

I do not believe that divorce was God's will for my life. I do not believe God wants marriages to break apart. But I do believe that when we are broken and hurting we discover a God who relates more closely to us than ever before. Thrust out into a sea of incomprehensible uncertainty, I decided to trust and rely fully on God's plan for my life.

My pain, suffering, and crisis was bringing me closer to God. On my knees in prayer and with my heart immersed in the words of faith, I was confident. My family had been stripped of its wholeness, but nothing would be able to separate me from the love of God. At that moment all that was certain was that God was with me, and His hand was very evident still in my life, not as a fifteen-year-old teenager, but as a hurting, wounded adult.

My wife, too, was the recipient of God's grace.

While I had lost a love, I was beginning to cling, in ever clearer ways, to a Love that would never let me go. I turned my weary soul over to Him and walked more intentionally into His life.

> O love that wilt not let me go,
> I rest my weary soul in thee:
> I give thee back the life I owe,
> That in thine ocean depths its flow
> May richer, fuller be.

O Cross that liftest up my head,
I dare not ask to fly from thee;
I lay in dust life's glory dead,
And from the ground there blossoms red
Life that shall endless be.

There it is! Our affirmation. The Cross. The loving embrace of God, that can lift up the defeated lives of people, who lie lost in the dusty dryness of the life that they have created for themselves. Lifted in the loving embrace of God. The greatest embrace any one of us can feel. Through it is released new life that shall endless be.

Shortly after this episode, I worshiped with Robert Schuller at the Crystal Cathedral in California. Norman Peale had just sent me Robert A. Schuller's book, *Getting Through the Going Through Stage,* which he wrote about his own divorce. Eagerly reading every word, I found much comfort in his journey.

But at the Communion service in the Crystal Cathedral I actually felt the loving touch and embrace of God. Bob and Arvelle Schuller embraced me at their home, on their front porch, praying for me as Bob held me in his strong arms. At the Communion service in the Cathedral I felt the total encouragement of God's presence.

Taking the bread in my hands and lifting the cup of wine to my lips I heard the words, "God will not hold our iniquities against us. As far as the East is from the West, He will separate our sins from us."

I had committed many iniquities, many indiscretions.

In that moment of His presence I knew what it meant to be forgiven, accepted, embraced, and loved by God. It is an embrace that binds, that can never be severed. It is a love that will not let you go.

To begin my healing process, I relinquished my anger and hatred, my feelings of inferiority stirred by a spouse's rejection, all that was bad within my mind about my wife. All that was bad within my own mind about myself. I gave it all to God. I wanted to leave that worship service as a child of God, beginning life anew in His footsteps and in His arms.

It was a moment of purging.

Standing, looking at the spot where I had just knelt, I bade farewell to an image of my former self. I left it there.

I turned around and felt the warmth of the California skies in a new way. Not only was God embracing me. I was embracing Him.

The embracing of the two is an embrace that binds.

CHAPTER 5

Of Birds, Blossoms, and Butterflies

"Look at the lilies of the fields, they neither toil nor do they spin. Even Solomon in all his glory is not arrayed as one of these. The birds of the air. They are not worried about planting seeds or gathering the harvest into the barn. Their heavenly Father knows of their need. And are you not worth more than a bird?"

[*Matt. 6:26–29, paraphrase*]

God knows your need! He sees you when you fall! Because He has created you, your life is significantly more worthy than the rest of creation manifesting His glory.

Are you suffering the pain of loss? Has life tossed you to the wind or thrown you out of the nest? Do you feel empty, lonely, or sad?

Encountering such feelings, we yearn for someone to embrace us, comfort us, and gather us in loving arms of confidence and hope. The tender, loving embrace of God is there for each of you because He knows your need.

The lilies of the fields, birds in the air, fallen sparrows. You! All expressive of the natural order of things. The truth is simply this. We are intricately woven into this loving fabric of God's creative love. As He sustains flowers, birds, butterflies, the world, He cares for us. We need to take the time to listen quietly to the way God reminds us of His loving presence in our lives. We are more worthy than a bird even though we find ourselves wounded and broken as birds tossed from their nests.

Why did God choose to include in His Word the beautiful scenes of lilies in the meadows of white narcissus and glowing buttercups, fields ablaze with poppies, or woods carpeted with bluebells, Queen Anne's lace, feathery tufts of cotton grass, and moss?

Why did God highlight, not only the fallen sparrow, held in His loving embrace, but eagles that mount up on wings, with the breath of His new life lifting them higher?

These were all ways of making us sensitive to the things in this world which delight us and Him. They were also to make us aware that He cared more for us than for anything else He created.

A walk through the woods reminds us of the great Creator. Songs of birds, hums of crickets, the rustle of leaves in gentle breezes, the ripple of water gently flowing over rocks—all these fill the air and our senses. At the ocean's edge the pounding, crashing crests of white-foamed waves convey the majesty of God's power and influence over all of life. The calming, persistent flow of the seas, grasping onto the sands like clinging, aspiring fingertips, reminds us of the never-relinquishing grasp of God upon our own lives.

The scent of crushed pine needles under foot, broken in crispness, penetrates our nostrils and conveys to us God's desire to make all of life fragrant with His love.

Richard Jefferies said,

> Resting quietly under an ash tree, with the scent of flowers, and the odour of green buds and leaves, a ray of sunlight yonder lighting up the lichen and the moss on the oak trunk, a gentle air stirring in the branches above, giving glimpses of fleecy clouds sailing in the sky above, there comes into the mind a feeling of intense joy in the simple fact of living.[1]

We discover here God's intention in telling us about birds, blossoms, and butterflies—to help us see beyond our own problems by placing into our minds and hearts an intense joy in the simple fact of living. We can thank God that we are alive, despite our experience of the moment. We can thank Him, knowing that He fully loves us, sustains us. Even the Psalm 23 provides the interplay between dark valleys and green pastures and living streams of water. We will be with Him forever. He will not let us fall.

These beautiful, natural experiences are not only places which provide us with enchantment. They are also moments to remind us that we are all part of the beauty. They help us to understand that there is joy in living, joy in being loved by God. We are a part of the birds, blossoms, and butterflies. God has created us. He knows our need.

It is devastating to be rejected, renounced, devalued by another human being. We want approval and affirmation. Our longing is to be accepted and loved. That is why the Bible affirms this loving embrace of God by saying,

Are you not worth more than the birds?

or

God so loved you that He sent His only
Son that you might have abundant life.

When, in the quiet woods, we find ourselves in touch with the voices of nature, we need to feel deeply in the quiet recesses of our hearts this message that God has for each of us. Our lives can be abundantly beautiful as the master's finger of creation touches us to wholeness. We need not remain wounded all of our lives. Remember, He gently picks up fallen sparrows. He will gently carry you.

OF BIRDS

Early in my theological training, God taught me a valuable lesson regarding the need to sustain people who have found their lives tossed to the wind, who are drifting aimlessly and floundering hopelessly, rejected and despised.

While I was a student at Wesley Theological Seminary in Washington, D.C., in the early seventies, my apartment on campus provided me with more than space for studying. I built an aviary in the corner of the bedroom to house seven bird cages and fourteen canaries. Their sweet song filled the apartment with music, making the dawn of morning a symphony as each bird answered the other's rich notes.

This apartment was often referred to as the most "seedy" apartment on campus because of the birdseed scattered beneath the cages. Much of my free time was spent studying these birds and watching them flutter about, building nests, laying eggs, and hatching new broods.

At evening the cages were draped in heavy black cloths to create a nocturnal illusion and to delay their early morning greeting to my often objecting groans and moans as I rolled over in bed and covered my ears with the pillows. These black cloths were a futile attempt, for even the night might be penetrated by the shrill cry of a bird that was stubbornly determined to stay awake. When morning broke, so did the seven voices of the male canaries.

Approaching the cage one morning for their weekly cleaning, I noticed one of the birds huddled in the corner of the aviary with its feathers ruffled, its luster and sheen subdued, shaking with all appearances of sickness.

"Lice!!"

This disease could destroy a whole brood.

The potential threat to the well-being of the other birds assisted me in immediately determining the fate of this infected bird.

I unscrewed the window screen to slide back the large glass windows. This frail, struggling creature was frightened as my hand intruded into the corner of the cage. Grasping the bird in my palm, with its pale, tiny head poking through my thumb and forefinger, with its glazed, beady eyes looking desperate, I extended my hand out the window.

Avoiding any glances at the bird, I thrust it into the air, releasing it, not to any freedom, but to its doom, to certain death in the natural elements. I tossed it to the wind. I was comfortable in not knowing how it would die, whether from the natural elements or from some feline waiting for its prey.

The brood was protected. I had only to sterilize the other cages. Placing them in steamy hot water in the bathroom tub, I was interrupted by a knock on the apartment door. An hour and a half had passed since the bird was released.

Grabbing a towel to dry my hands, I walked over and opened the front door.

"Cadmus, you have canaries, don't you?"

"Yes, why?" I asked.

"Come out here quickly."

Hoping not to find what my suspicions were leading me to fear, I ran with him onto the lawn. Under the tree, another classmate held his hand over a shoe box in the deep grass.

Cautiously lifting the box, I found myself staring eye to eye with the canary I had tossed to the wind.

"Is it yours?"

In embarrassment I said, "Looks familiar. Let me check."

Running breathlessly back into the apartment ahead of my friends who were quickly tracing my steps, I awkwardly unhinged the cage doors to create the appearance that this bird's escape was accidental.

The hands that had quickly tossed the bird to the wind now gently reached into the box. In tenderness, those same hands clasped the palsied bird and placed it back on the bottom of the cage, restoring it to the brood,

The bird and I stood eye to eye. I in disbelief. The bird with a look of "you thought you'd get rid of me, huh?"

Not having the nerve to release it again, I half-heartedly nursed it the best I could.

After several days a change in the color and luster of its feathers was obvious. It was fluffy, regaining the sheen of a brightly active canary. First balancing itself on a lower perch, it regained strength until it courageously jumped from perch to perch, gliding on the swing to the tune of the clearest song ever projected from its throat.

Its recovery was miraculous. I learned my lesson, a lesson specifically designed by God. I had tossed one of God's creatures, hurting, struggling, and ill, to the wind. It was easier to rid myself of the problem than to commit myself to its healing and renewal.

God, who was calling me to serve and dedicate my life to

his people, was teaching me a lesson. I learned, not from a theological textbook or in an academic setting, but in an apartment building complex, through a wounded bird that regained its strength and was restored to life.

And God said, "Cadmus, never treat my children as you have treated this frail, sickly bird."

For are not people worth more than this little bird?

I learned about the dignity of human beings through understanding God's love for a little bird. Never again would I pitch, fling, or dispose of any of God's tiniest creatures or hurting human beings as I had done to this suffering canary.

One day it happened to me, this pain of rejection. The door of my home was opened, and my injured, broken life was tossed to the wind out of a home that was breaking apart. I was left emotionally suspended in a cold world of fear and uncertainty. I was now the wounded bird. I was frightened of the world into which I was tossed, wondering what experiences would prey on my emotions.

The gospel truth, however, became more crystallized. Are we not more than birds? Does not God know our need? Will not His loving embrace catch us when life's cruelties disperse us into the frightening unknown?

The important lesson I learned was not only one of treating God's creation with respect—or another human being with kindness and love—but also that, in my own uncertainty and doubt, fear and anxiety, I must never toss myself away. I must never neglect my own integrity and well-being under life's adversities. I needed to learn to take care of myself. I would never toss myself away, except to toss my life into the loving, caring embrace of God.

As the gospel hymn proclaims, "His eye is on the sparrow, and I know He watches me."

It is difficult to affirm this when so many obstacles confront us in life, when we are wounded, hurt, and tossed carelessly into hopelessness by an unsympathizing world.

I was alone and cut off. My life was a pathetic shambles. The words from Psalm 88 penetrated my despair with the hopelessness it so poignantly expresses:

> For my soul is full of troubles,
> And my life draws near to the grave.
> I am counted with those who go down to the pit;
> I am like a man who has no strength,
> Adrift among the dead,
> Like the slain who lie in the grave,
> Whom You remember no more,
> And who are cut off from Your hand.
> . . . .
> LORD, I have called daily upon You;
> I have stretched out my hands to You.
> Will You work wonders for the dead?
> Shall the dead arise *and* praise You?[2]

So many people are tossed and abandoned like wounded birds. I could not understand why my own wife could not work with me or help me through my suffering.

There are so many who cannot handle the suffering and pain of others and so they remove themselves from the pain and the potential of being healing agents. Unable to handle pain, we run from it. Unable to care for others, we have the tendency to toss them. In his book *Reaching Out,* Henri Nouwen speaks of the need for compassionate love for those who are hurting: "Those who do not run away from our pains but touch them with compassion bring healing and new strength. The paradox indeed is that the beginning of healing is in the solidarity with the pain."[3]

To be abandoned and shunned is one of life's greatest pains. Beyond the despairing words of the psalmist in Psalm 88 is God's loving embrace. There is Easter after Good Friday. God makes Himself one with your journey of life, even when all others desert you. You can find comfort and strength in His embrace.

Another bird story will highlight this point.

Frank Baum's immortal classic *The Wizard of Oz,* in which Judy Garland played young Dorothy, begins with a scene of a breathless Dorothy, hysterically confronting Auntie Em and Uncle Henry with Miss Gulch's plans to destroy her pet dog Toto.

Auntie Em and Uncle Henry, seemingly uninterested in

Dorothy's plight, are preoccupied with a broken down incubator, which is threatening the survival of the brood of yellow chicks.

The scene is one of chaos, both in Dorothy's fear over Toto's safety and in her aunt and uncle's desperation to save the baby chicks. Auntie Em brushes Dorothy off with a suggestion to "go away" and find a place where she won't get into any trouble! Auntie Em appears overwhelmed by her own personal crisis. But she does remind all of us today to find a place in life that is safe from trouble.

The incubator is out of commission. The chicks need warm security to survive. Dorothy is frightened, needing loving reassurance that no harm will come to Toto, a pet that represents her whole world.

The scene is a reminder that we cannot depend upon life to provide our security. Life is constantly threatened. Our security is tenuous.

When a simple incubator malfunctions or some invention of great technology fails, we discover that life is not dependable. But the source of life is. God can sustain you when you are thrust into trouble. The psalmist, after he was able to see beyond abandonment, was able to say, "God, you are my help in time of trouble."

Amidst all the anxiety, fears, confusions, and frustrations of life comes the calm resolve of Auntie Em's wise understanding about life's preservation. She lifts each fluffy ball, each tender yellow chick, and shoves them under the warm feathers of brooding hens.

While Dorothy seeks to find the place where she won't get into any trouble and dreams of a place over the rainbow, Auntie Em deals with her frantic emergency and returns the chicks to their natural setting—under the hens. Before the invention of the incubator, the chicks had a natural place of security and survival, under the wings of hens, where they were nurtured and where they could grow.

Under the hen. Beneath the security of the wings of the hen. Yes, Dorothy lifts her eyes to see the promise over the rainbow. And we need always to lift our eyes above our problems to see God's promises. But also, while Dorothy looks over the rainbow, Auntie Em reminds us to look under God's tender wings for security.

Without placing ourselves under God's care we are left desolate. Matthew 23:37–39 says,

"O Jerusalem, Jerusalem, the one who kills the prophets and stones those who are sent to her! How often I wanted to gather your children together, as a hen gathers her chicks under *her* wings, but you were not willing! See! Your house is left to you desolate; for I say to you, you shall see Me no more till you say, 'Blessed is He who comes in the name of the LORD.'"

As I look at the last days I lived at home and see the unwillingness of a couple to allow God to gather us under His wings in our time of trouble, I see why the collapse of our relationship was inevitable. "See! Your house is left to you desolate." My marriage, my home, lay in ruin. We could not bring ourselves to find hope under the loving wings of God.

Remember, though, there is much more than abandonment beyond the sentiments expressed in Psalm 88. There is a God who brings us under His wings. Our healing comes in His solidarity with our pain. He shares in the experience of our brokenness.

We see it made explicitly clear in the opening scene of this immortal *Wizard of Oz*. As a hen gathers her chicks under her wings, so does God gather his children unto Himself. At the end of this classic movie, we come to a full expression of what it means to be placed under God's wings. Dorothy's last words in the movie are these: "Oh, Auntie Em, there's no place like home!!" As people of faith, we must look to God and say, "Oh, God, there is no place like home—under Your wings!"

Perhaps your marriage has failed. But God does not fail.

Perhaps life has filled you with fear. But God's love casts out fear.

You might be feeling abandoned and shunned. No one can understand your pain or identify with it or take the time to relate to it. But God knows. He will not leave you alone.

Maybe your life is bleak and uneventful. God sent to you His Son, Jesus Christ, that you might have an abundant, joyous life.

Is there a relationship in your life that has cooled because the embrace in which once love was incubated is just not radiating warmth anymore? God can take the heart of stone and create a heart warm with love—if you let Him.

Let God lift you and restore you. See the cross always as the holy sign shaping your life. God is an indwelling sympathizer. He comforts because He has compassion.

The psalmist said, "In the shadow of His wings I will sing for joy." Under His wings He will sustain you, giving you dignity, self-respect, courage, and comforting love. Claim the assurance of His love for you. Trust Him as He places you under His care. See the possibilities He has for your life as you safely abide in Him.

> Under His wings I am safely abiding;
> Though the night deepens and tempests are wild,
> Still I can trust Him; I know He will keep me;
> He has redeemed me, and I am His child.

> Under His wings, under His wings,
> Who from His love can sever?
> Under His wings my soul shall abide,
> Safely abide forever.

God's loving embrace is the only reliable condition of life. Trust it. Embrace God. Let His wings embrace you.

OF BLOSSOMS

> For there is hope for a tree,
> If it is cut down, that it will sprout again,
> And that its tender shoots will not cease.
> Though its root may grow old in the earth,
> And its stump may die in the ground,
> *Yet* at the scent of water it will bud
> And bring forth branches like a plant.[4]

This affirmation of new life reminds us of the way Christ compares us to nature. Even though Job was despairing, Christ reminds us that while there is hope for a tree, there is also hope for our own lives. Consider the lilies of the field; they neither toil nor spin.

The Anglo-French base of the noun *toil* means to struggle and be overwhelmed with turmoil in an exhausting effort just to stay alive. It denotes a painful and exhausting intensity of labor. It makes of life drudgery that depletes us until we are weary or disgusted with living.

At the "scent of water" the potential of growth can emerge even out of the oldest dead stump.

The love of God constantly offers to us refreshing hope. We can blossom once again with a vital enthusiasm for living.

Why then, do so many despair like Job, especially when we know of the gospel power and the promise that our shepherd Lord will constantly lead us by streams of living water?

When life seems to cut us down, we need only turn to Isaiah 42:3 to be provided with our answer of hope:

> A bruised reed He will not break,
> and smoking flax He will not quench. . . .

God will never leave you broken. Why? Because He sent His Son to remind us that no heart is so heavy or so broken that it cannot be healed or lifted. No life is so lonely or desolate that He will not restore it to light and life through His loving embrace. God does not snuff out life. He gives the believer eternal life.

Romans says His love is a "hope which does not disappoint because the love of God has been poured out within our hearts through the Holy Spirit."

In John Steinbeck's short story "The Chrysanthemums," we discover how the premature pruning of a plant often promotes its blossoming at a later time, even though the pruning results in the necessary pain of cutting off buds which are just about ready to open.

With a woman bent over a flowerbed, with hands carefully and intentionally pruning the new buds, John Steinbeck unfolds a story of growth that comes from pain: "She picked up the little pile of shoots she had prepared. With her strong fingers she pressed them into the sand and tamped around them with her knuckles."[5] The woman explains how she carefully cultivates the marvelous variety of colorful flowers to her curious neighbor who is leaning over the fence in conversation: "It's the budding that takes the most care. It's when you're picking off the buds you don't want. Everything goes right down into your fingertips. You watch your fingers work. They pick and pick the buds. They never make a mistake. They know."[6]

Often when I work in my garden, I sense a twinge of reluctance to cut back, prune, or especially pick off the buds just when they are about ready to bloom. I want to see the blossoms as quickly as possible, rather than follow the procedure required for the full strengthening and nourishment of the shrub or flower.

Each time I pick off a bud I know its pain from images in Steinbeck's "The Chrysanthemums." The feeling of it goes right down "into my fingertips, into my whole body." But look at what is said in an affirming way in this horticultural process: "They pick and pick the buds, these fingers, but they never make a mistake. They know."[7]

And so does God never make a mistake in His pruning, shaping, and designing of our lives. His hands, His gentle fingertips, as they touch us, never make a mistake. He knows what He is doing in our lives.

There is nothing more devastating than the pruning of a loved one from your life through death.

We are pruned each time we are called into the boss's office to find our job has been terminated.

We know the pain of rebellious children cutting off their loyalties from us through anger and resentment.

We feel the emotional separation from a marriage's premature collapse before any cultivation of the ground was possible or even attempted to enrich the soil of faith and enable couples and families to survive.

Illnesses, like a thief in the night, completely alter our plans for living. The diagnosis of cancer becomes like harsh mutilating fingertips, pruning away the life that once had so much potential.

Like Job we say in our despair, "When we are cut down we die."

In all of life's prunings, however, we discover God's ability to allow His fingertips to do their intentional work. Remember, God makes no mistakes. And our lives will be made richer, fuller, and more beautiful, even though the feeling of being prematurely cut down causes us to become despondent.

God's hands are planting hands. New seeds of life are always infusing our lives with energy for growth and capacity for beauty. God's tender hands continue to plant a new seed, a new miracle inside you.

No matter what life does to you, you can become an exciting, beautiful, wonderful person.

Tennyson said,

> Flower in the crannied wall,
> I pluck you out of the crannies,
> I hold you here, root and all, in my hand,
> Little flower—but *if* I could understand
> What you are, root and all, and all in all,
> I should know what God and man is.

Oh, only if we could know and understand what God has in mind for our own lives as He holds us in His hands. We might be able to handle more easily the struggles of the soul. Only to know what His plan is, who we are, "root and all, and all in all." But then we would know fully who God is.

What we need to learn in life, as we journey through it, is to understand that God's love, expressed through His fingertips touching our lives, is a love that will not make mistakes. If we are stretching from the pruning, the process is all in God's shaping.

If your life is unsettled, perhaps you need to take a look at those tender hands of His, those fingertips, and realize that He never makes a mistake. He knows your need and it might just be that your upset and confusion are the result of the process of His hands, tilling the soil of your soul or picking off the weak bud that has not blossomed yet.

Remember, God's hands know what they are doing. Place your hands in His and trust His loving embrace.

Gardening is a therapeutic hobby for me. Immersed in the soil, surrounded by the loveliness of nature, I escape the stresses of life in the aromatic fragrances of nature. To be in the soil, to tenderly touch the pastel petals of flowers, is to be touched by divinity. Just looking at a cluster of forget-me-nots, is to be reminded that God will never forget me. It is unfortunate that we think the only purpose of the color, scent, and honey of flowers is to attract insects so that pollination will guarantee the perennial array of splendor.

Jesus introduced us to the lilies of the fields so that we could begin to understand God's perennial love for our lives. We can see played out in our lives God's creative fingertips, dusting us with the pollen of His grace. That is why the lilies did not toil nor spin. God's fingertips took care of them. His hands will sustain you also.

During a fall season, I planted a flower bed of some six hundred tulip bulbs along the garden pathway leading to our home. It was designed to create a border that would blossom later that spring in brilliant crimsons, pinks, and yellows.

As the first new shoots broke through the encrusted earth after winter's thaw, I began watching their growth each day with joyous anticipation. Daily they appeared to grow before my eyes, stretching their unfolding blades skyward. Tightly formed buds began to appear in the center of the green blades at the bases of the stems. Day after day, I greeted them with tender care, envisioning them in full bloom. They were a source of pride and joy, to me and to the neighborhood.

Sarah, my youngest daughter, at the time fourteen months old, spent many happy moments with me in the garden. She had her own plastic bright red, yellow, and green garden tools. Father and daughter, in soil and sun, shared hours of joy. Warm, spring days present occasions to talk together about God's beautiful world.

The anticipation of these radiant blossoms twinkled in her eyes also. She knew something spectacular was about to happen.

Each day as she strayed into areas of the flowerbeds where little feet could cause extensive damage, I firmly reminded her that appropriate distance was necessary. So she learned to lean over the flower buds just enough to smell them and say, "Smell, pretty!" Each day she walked through the garden, tugging at my side, pointing to the flowers, and said, "Smell, pretty!"

I was proud of my green thumb and gloried in the accolades of the many neighbors who came to express their marvel over the six hundred brilliant flowers reaching twenty-four inches skyward, pulling in the rays of the sun with their petals.

One afternoon in the garden when I became preoccupied with transferring pieces of shrubbery, Sarah began one of her escapades, an adventure which set no boundaries for her curiosity.

By the time I turned my attention to her, she had placed her diaper-padded bottom in a bed of tulip bulbs, now crushed beneath her. Several red tulip petals protruded from the corners of her broad smile.

Speechless and infuriated, I swung her out from among the tulips onto a pile of grass clippings. Tulip petals now gone from her lips, she was spitting out grass cuttings.

One, two, ten, fourteen, fifteen, twenty, twenty-two tulip bulbs. Pulled out of the ground, stems ripped from the bulbs.

Tears welled up in my eyes. The carefully planned flower bed had just been devastated by a pair of "luvs." I felt no "luv" for her at the moment. Sarah sensed my fear and anger. She did not know what she should do—laugh or cry.

In an attempt to soothe my anger, Sarah picked up a broken stem, extending the flower toward me, saying with half a smile and a slight tear running down her cheek, "Smell, pretty?"

Frustration overshadowed any compassion for her. Grabbing the yellow, green, and red plastic garden tools, I slammed them in her bucket and marched them into the garage, placing them out of her reach. With hands on my hips, I stood before my garden in defeat. I was more concerned about my flowers than the beautiful little creation standing next to me and frightened by what my actions might be.

"Smell, pretty!!??"

Through misty eyes I saw a frightened little child before me. Yet all that concerned me were my flowers. It took all of my control to keep me from yelling, "Get lost!!!" at an uncomprehending toddler.

Again, "Smell, pretty!?"

It was then that I realized it. Sarah did not see the damage she had caused. She grasped the beauty of exquisite, colorful, fragrant tulips. I was gripped by anger and frustration. The contrast was startling.

"God, help me with my anger," I prayed.

"Help me to see not the damage created by a curious fourteen-month-old child but the beauty of life through her eyes."

This calming prayer provided an opportunity for resolve. Through it I perceived a redeeming element.

Returning to the tool shed, I picked up a pair of pruning shears and Sarah's garden tools. Sarah joined me and we knelt in the wide patch of dark earth made naked by the removed tulips. We began gathering all the broken stems. Placing Sarah's hand on the handles of the pruning shears and wrapping my huge, dirty palms around hers, I helped her to cut the remaining bent blades and blossoms until we held twenty-two tulip bulbs. Before us now, at the most visible area in my garden, was a large empty, barren, once beautifully adorned, open patch of black earth.

Sarah followed me into the house. We snipped the bottom of each stem and placed it in the vase. With each insertion, Sarah held the flower to her nose and then to mine and said, "Smell, pretty!" In a few moments there stood before us the most beautiful bouquet of spring flowers. And beside me, with a gleam in her eyes, was one radiant little child. I was not certain which was more beautiful and lovely.

I lifted Sarah up in my arms, and she leaned over the vase and said, "Smell, pretty!"

Imagine, anger subsided and a redeeming quality in this situation was found. Together, we placed the flowers on the center of the dining room table. For over two weeks we shared our family dinner at this table, with twenty-two tulips as our floral centerpiece. Each night, during our blessing for the meal, Sarah's voice penetrated the room with the words, "Smell, pretty!"

I learned through blossoms that He will not allow a bruised reed to remain broken. There were tender fingertips evident in the plucking of these flowers. I thank God that He allowed me to realize this. Who would ever have thought that through the destruction of a flower bed, through the premature plucking of these glorious blossoms, God would create a centerpiece of joy? The real joy was that God was able to exchange my anger for love.

The lesson was this. Had I remained angry and become abrupt in my actions to Sarah, would this little girl have grown to fear her father? Fear his uncontrolled anger? Would I have planted another kind of seed, one that would not have blossomed into a beautiful flower, but one in the mind of a child who would have grown to be unappreciative of God's spectacular creation around her?

Oh yes, you can be assured that I kept a watchful eye on her each time we found ourselves in the garden again. But a seed was planted in my own heart that day. It was planted there by a little child to whom I would always give my life and love so that she could go through life, look at it, and know that this is the creation that God made for her. So that she could rejoice fully in God's world and in those she loves and say, "Smell, pretty!"

The beauty of that garden and our home has been stunted, somewhat, by a divorce that has prematurely cut our family relationship. Could we have grown into something more splendid and beautiful had we cultivated our relationship or had we allowed the tender fingers of God to prune us, weeding out that which became weed infested, or even if we had worked harder at tilling the soil of our encrusted relationship?

And so, a barren spot is exposed in our family. Lives are uprooted. Browned edges fringe the once-beautiful flowers of our lives.

It's hard at a time like this to look at life and say, "Smell, pretty!"

But God will take that which is broken and bruised in all of our lives and form a centerpiece of His creation, in which He will place all of his love and hope.

He can still make life fragrant with hope and reflective of his goodness, kindness, and glory. Your lives can still be warmed by the golden sunshine and refreshed by the rain He provides. To this we owe the greenness of new life that is God's constant provision.

Yes, we all go through situations which can bruise us. We are all broken from time to time. Remember though, "a bruised reed He will not break." You will still blossom and grow. Tomorrow is a new day and a new life. God always places the scent of water in your life, living streams, the kind which will free us from thirst forever.

A song made popular by Bette Midler entitled *The Rose*, captures the essence of what I am saying:

> When the night has been too lonely
> And the road has been too long,
> And you think that love is only
> For the lucky and the strong,
> Just remember in the winter,
> Far beneath the bitter snows,
> Lies the seed that with the sun's love
> In the spring becomes the rose.[8]

There will always be new life for you. Even if you have to wait for spring. Trust His fingertips. They never make mistakes.

OF BUTTERFLIES

No one can give a definition of the soul. But we know what it feels like. The soul is the sense of something higher than ourselves, something that stirs in us thoughts, hopes, and aspirations which go out to the world of goodness, truth, and beauty. The soul is a burning desire to breathe in this world of light and never lose it—to remain children of light.

—Albert Schweitzer
Reverence For Life

The Sunday I announced my eventual divorce to my congregation was a day of emotional collapse and fear. Standing before a crowd of worshipers, who had up to this moment viewed us as epitomizing an ideal love, was a traumatic moment in which the flaws about to be shared would reveal imperfection. It was perhaps the first time in my ministry with this congregation that they would perceive me as real and vulnerable.

At the very depth of my anxiety, my daughter Sarah was to stir something higher within me later that day. When I was so low, something brighter; when all was bleak, something good; when I was filled with the guilt of contributing to the deterioration of a relationship and to the hurt of a woman I had loved immensely. Like Albert Schweitzer, Sarah pointed out a beauty and a truth which lit up a life that seemed so dim.

The choir had just finished their anthem and the congregation was seated after singing the hymn before the message. Hearts were opened for a message of faith and inspiration. I needed to be open, forthright, and honest with my people, who had grown to love my family with an unshifting loyalty.

With head bowed, I prayed for confidence and emotional constraint. This loving setting would allow me to be real with my feelings and true to my own pain. My only suspicion was my ability to remain calm.

Trusting God to radiate the love of the gospel through the personal suffering I was about to share, I announced my divorce to the controlled shock of the congregation. The Board of Elders and Deacons, already aware of this marital crisis, were a bulwark of strength and confidence as their eyes expressed their love.

Laurie was attending church with me, sitting with a few friends in whom she always found trusting confidence. Her eyes were stalwart in her love for me, yet her tears revealed a hurting little girl, hurting for herself and for me. There was an affinity between us. In one brief glance, she discovered that my tears were reflection pools of her daddy's inner fears, hurts, and pain for himself and an emotional conveyance of hope and love for her.

Preaching this sermon was a difficult hurdle. The stillness in the congregation permitted, in an intense way, the presence of the Spirit to lift us all in God's loving care and embrace.

An image of a butterfly came to mind, not as any prepared part of my manuscript but as an unfolding message from my heart. In its story, the discovery was made once again of God's ability to teach us about life through nature, lilies of the field, birds of the air, and butterflies.

I wanted to close my message with something sweet in its imagery, lovely in its sentiment, to provide a peaceful quiet to the lives I had just disturbed. We all needed a ray of sunlight, something to refresh our spirits. And so the story of a butterfly came to mind, a message that would later lift me higher than my problem and stir within me a thought of hope and aspiration. It would be God's revelation to me that my world would still be one of goodness, truth, and beauty.

Often, while I work in the garden, watering the flowers and shrubs, a curious butterfly, freely gyrating from blossom to blossom, is lured by the scent of flowers, unaware in its seeking of pollen encased in drops of morning dew, that I am nearby, with garden hose in hand, ready to chase it with the pulsating flow of water.

Fluttering its wings in midair, it didn't know the nozzle was in hot pursuit of its fanciful flight, to weigh its wings down with moisture. The heavier the wings became, the more strenuously it tried to soar in a free-spirited flight. As it sought retreat in the underbrush of nearby shrubbery, I persistently pursued it with the hose, with the nozzle turned now only to a slight mist of water. But that was enough to cause the butterfly to fall to the mud puddles at the roots of the bushes. Its slowed opening and closing of wings clearly indicated this little creature was exhausted.

I seldom do this. Occasionally, I did it as play.

This Sunday morning, as I stood in my pulpit using the image of the butterfly, it was my own spirit now that was trying to rise above my problem, struggling to take flight, to lift myself above the pressures of life that were hitting me forcefully as if all of life had turned its oppressive nozzle of burden and care on me.

My once joyous spirit was drenched with care and trouble. Oppression overwhelmed my spirit. I was grievously and severely dejected. It was a time for my people to be pastor to me, to pray for me, to love me, to share my pain.

As I once threw a wounded bird out of my apartment window, I now also knew what it meant to have the wings of my spirit coated heavily with the burden of the greatest problem life had ever placed upon me.

Here I stood, wanting the living streams of life to flow within me, to lift me, to spray God's whispered hope upon my heart. I wanted to open my wings so that God could support me. My soul had been weary and fainting for weeks. Surviving this service was made possible by two things: God's loving embrace and the loving embrace of my people.

Later that day, I basked in the sun in my back yard, in the warm respite of gentle spring breezes, trying to touch a new word of hope, catch a new moment of a strength, gain a clearer perspective of who I was. Little Sarah, who had not been at church that morning and therefore was unaware of the images of the morning message, came to the lounge chair where I was asleep.

Pushing me on the shoulder she said, "Daddy, look!"

I ignored her.

She persisted, shoving my shoulder and shouted even louder, *"Daddy! Look!!!"*

"What, Sarah?" I said, quickly sitting up in my chair.

"Look, Daddy—over there!"

"Where?"

"Right here."

"At what?" I was puzzled.

She said, "Right here. There's a butterfly."

"Where?" I exclaimed. Was she pointing to something I was missing?

"Right here, Daddy!"

And she waved her finger in a circle in front of the two of us, moving the empty space with the flow of her hands. Before us was an invisible, imaginary butterfly.

At this moment the Spirit of God touched me. I pulled Sarah into the warm embrace of my arms, and the precious gift of our embrace moved me to tears. For she showed me something I could not see with my own eyes, nor feel because of my own pain and hurt. She put me in touch with my soul. With God. With the presence of Christ.

She did for me what Albert Schweitzer said in *Reverence for Life*. She created a sense of something higher than ourselves, something that stirs in us thoughts, hopes, and aspirations that go out into the world of goodness, truth, and beauty. She became a child of light for me.

The loving embrace of God provides for each of us something we cannot see with our own eyes. This embrace lifts us up higher than ourselves and stirs hope and faith within us. And so God creates within us the burning desire to find the embrace that will never let us go.

The loving embrace of Christ on the cross, drawing all of

us to Himself, is the Spirit of life that lifts us closer to the king-dom, making us all children of light, opening our wings of faith so that we can soar in the Spirit. Grasp the cross, and the light of life will fill you. Hold on, and you will always be a child of light.

CHAPTER 6

Embrace Faith And Be Strong

*F*aith can make you strong! You can grasp this faith as you embrace the life-changing power of the cross. In this cross you will discover life's greatest power for living.

A visit to my cousins Ruth Ann and Michael at the Schofield Barracks Army Base in Hawaii, provided me with a spiritual encounter along the Pacific Island Coastal region of the Polynesian Islands. These relatives arranged my entrance into restricted governmental territory.

Boarding an army jeep for the jolting ride along rugged mountain paths, we arrived at the crest of the restricted Kole Kole Pass overlooking the sultry seas of Hawaii. The vista was breathtaking, with tropical fragrances of lush exotic flowers and rich, humid dirt, damp from the early morning misty clouds.

On December 7, 1941, Kole Kole Pass formed the basin between two mountain peaks through which unannounced enemy planes came and destroyed our ships and the precious lives of our soldiers at both Schofield Barracks and Pearl Harbor, thrusting America into World War II. My cousins and I stood in taciturn reflection, our thoughts interrupted only by the echoes of this day of infamy.

The ride to Kole Kole Pass was not intended to show the

route by which the enemy silently approached our sleeping troops that early morning in December, but to show me a magnificent tribute to the lives of the thousands who died. At the top of the hill, overlooking the valley into a sea of infinity, was a magnificent forty-foot-high, white, steel monument. Surrounding the structure was a fence. As Michael unlocked the gate, my eyes slowly rose to see towering above me in the blue, cloudless skies a white cross.

GRASP THE CROSS AND BE STRONG

Opening a small access door at the bottom of the cross, I saw a narrow ladder to the top, enabling the grounds superintendent to change the air traffic control lights.

I entered the cramped passageway, my shoulders touching the inside edges of the cross. These were close quarters, but there was a symbolic comfort in its secure embrace.

Grabbing the ladder, I began my ascent to the top, looking upward to protect myself from the phobia of heights. The interior of the cross created a wind tunnel, for from the opened door at the bottom a flow of tropic warmth circulated around my body as I climbed higher and higher. At the top, I pushed open the small door. The wind blew my hair uncontrollably around my face, whipping my shirt sleeves and creating a feeling of unsteadiness. I clung tightly to the cross.

The wind created the powerful presence of the Holy Spirit. Imagine the powerful mystical feeling of being inside a cross.

Through the cross I looked at the wide space of forever—the blue seas.

If we could go through life, clutching the cross, then no matter what happened to us, whatever unexpected crisis, pain, or threatening enemies life sent our way, we could remain strong. Our faith would make us sturdy in the face of a world that tries to weaken us. No adversity would overwhelm us as long as we were held in the cross' embrace.

Jesus said, "If you live in me, I will live in you."

Here, inside this cross, I felt that Christ was within me and I within him. Within this cross I found the loving embrace that is life's greatest power for living.

Second Corinthians 13:3 says that Christ is "not weak toward you, but mighty in you." You can embrace Christ and His cross and grasp life's greatest power for living. Christ can love you to wholeness and restore you to faith.

After many years of being hospitalized in Manhattan State Hospital for schizophrenia, Cynthia wrote me a letter which attests to the power of Christ in her life. She has survived because of God's loving embrace:

> Today, in church, I told you that your prayers for me are greatly appreciated. This is why. For the past seventeen years I have been repeatedly hospitalized with a mental disorder called acute chronic schizophrenia. At the back of my mind is the nightmarish fear that someday I will be committed to Manhattan State Hospital, a grim institution on Ward's Island. Your church is a haven of solace for me, and your living prayers are winged messages to God that I know are heard. Your spiritual support is priceless.
>
> Ever since I became a member of this all embracing church, I have not felt alone. The presence of Jesus Christ illuminates the sanctuary. I have experienced a feeling of exhilaration after listening to the choir sing and have come to think of Jesus as a friend because of your sermons. Many members of this spiritual family have reached out to me with comforting acceptance. I belong here.

Cynthia discovered a faith that has made her life strong. Her weak emotions have been embraced by the love of God. His touch has healed her. It is not a weak Christ she worships but a Christ of power. His embrace has strengthened and renewed her life. The power of God within her fragile life has given her wounded and lame spirit a sense of hope and healing. In our congregation she is a living witness to this simple truth: "If anyone *is* in Christ, *he is* a new creation."[1] This is the power of the Gospel. It can be your power for living if you let its message embrace you. Just place your life within the cross.

THE LAME MAN GRASPS FAITH

For forty years he sat at the roadside just outside the entrance of the city, at a gate called Beautiful. He was a pathetic, lame man longing to capture the essence of meaning for life. For four decades his supplication was for wholeness.

His hope was never affirmed until the disciples Peter and John intersected his life with the gift needed to heal his wounded spirit and life. This ideal spirit suddenly made the once-distant healing within touch and thought.

As it was his practice to beg for alms, Peter and John heard his solicitations as they crossed the threshold of Beautiful Gate. The surprising miracle for the lame man was to be the discovery of the cross at the threshold of Beautiful Gate. For something beautiful was going to adorn his life with grace.

Expecting a handout from Peter and John, he stretched his hands out urgently. In his begging for forty years, he had squatted in valueless human despair. But this day he was to be embraced by new life.

Instead of alms placed within his hands he hears these words from Peter: "Silver and gold I do not have, but what I do have I give you. . . ."[2]

What was this, "what I do have"? The lame man reached out and received Jesus' healing touch. Peter and John were the love of Christ, embracing all those who needed wholeness.

Peter and John embodied the life-changing love of Jesus. When the lame man touched Peter and John he grasped faith! He was embraced by God's love. They had no silver and gold. The greatest love in life was their only possession. They embraced the man with this gift of life at Beautiful Gate. They shared with him Jesus Christ's love.

To the amazement of all who knew him, he began leaping, walking, and he entered the temple praising God.

The disciples said, "And His name, through faith in His name, has made this man strong. . . ."[3]

After this miraculous recovery we observe the lame man restored to complete agility, walking along the road with Peter and John. His hand is tightly grasping their shoulder. For strength? For support? To stabilize his unsteady walk?

Why did he need the support of their shoulders since in the previous verses we have witnessed him becoming a man, who through the power of God, was able to stand firm on his two feet, to leap in joy, suspended in the midair of ecstasy? Running into the temple to praise God! He was literally a man transformed from lameness to dancing with joy!

What security did Peter and John provide?

Was he holding on to them because he needed stability? Was he uncertain and untrusting of the miracle performed within his life? Was there a chance that this was merely a fleeting, short-lived experience, a dream from which he was soon to awaken?

No!

He found the secret. He discovered the answer of power for living. The power came in the encounter with the embracing love of God. It was an embraceable love manifested in the love of two men, Peter and John. If he could continue to grasp on to them, on to the Jesus within them, he would possess a faith that would make him strong.

Here is the mystery he discerned: ". . . . Christ in you, the hope of glory."[4] The New Testament book of Colossians also says: "I want them to be in good heart and in the unity of love and to come to the full wealth of conviction which understanding brings, and grasp [embrace] God's secret" (NEB).[5] The lame man found the secret of his new life. He "grasped" and embraced that secret and brought Jesus into his life. At Beautiful Gate, the beautiful love of God became real for him.

Every one of us, at some point in our lives, will find ourselves standing at Beautiful Gate, asking for a quality of life, a gift from life that will sustain us, if not fulfill us. Such that God is, in all His loving care, you will find Him embracing you with all that will refresh your spirit.

His embrace is love in fullness, a love filled with Christ. This faith will *renew* your life, *heal* your life. It has the power to *restore* your life. The joy of this faith is knowing that through its power you can be *forgiven*.

FAITH CAN RENEW YOUR LIFE

To embrace a strong faith can provide you with peace of mind. This peace will renew your life. Peace of mind, as Ruskin beautifully observes, "must come in its own time, as the waters settle themselves into clearness as well as quietness; you can no more filter your mind into purity than you can compress it into calmness; you must keep it pure if you would have it pure, and throw no stones into it if you would have it quiet."[6]

It is the cross within your life, the loving embrace of God through Jesus Christ, that keeps you pure, calm, clear, and quiet. This loving embrace of God is what each of us needs to place within our lives, to heal them and to restore our souls.

Epictetus said,

> The soul is a much better thing than all the others which you possess. Can you then show me in what way you have taken care of it? For it is not likely that you, who are so wise a man, inconsiderately and carelessly allow the most valuable thing that you possess to be neglected and to perish.

Is it well with your soul? If your life filled with peace? Are you constantly renewing your life to purity? Are you leaving your life open for the working of God within, at His own time, allowing Him to strengthen, to renew, your life?

Or are you inconsiderate and careless of the most valuable tool for life that God has given to you—your faith?

Flying out West for a speaking engagement, I was seated at the window of the plane overlooking the wide expanse of clouds which formed a white carpet.

Seated next to me was an employee of the airline company. We were three-quarters of an hour into the flight when I began a conversation with Lewis about the current best-seller he was reading, *Eat to Win.*

Having just lost forty-two pounds myself through a concentrated weight reduction program, I felt that I could at least hold an intelligent conversation on diets.

As our snack was served by the stewardess, I took the opportunity to ask him, "Are you eating to win? You on a diet?" The conversation was superficial at first, each of us sharing our disciplined dieting programs. Our dialog slowly moved to Lewis' question of what I did for a living.

"I'm a minister in Manhattan!"

"You're pulling my leg!" he said in surprise as if in disbelief he discovered himself seated next to a man of faith.

"Sure am. I'm one of the ministers of the Collegiate Church of New York."

"Norman Vincent Peale's church?"

"Yes, I'm one of his colleagues! Do you know the church?"

With his reply, "I read all of his material," our conversation thrust forward at full throttle.

Lewis began sharing his feelings about how insignificant he had felt through the years. He was an altar boy in a Catholic church for many years. But he became discouraged with the "organized church," having received no support from it during some of the most critical, life-threatening developments of his life.

Abandoned by his parents, who felt his alcoholism would result in his complete degradation, he found himself confronted by a world that had no faith in him, saw no bright future for him. Even the church had no listening ear.

As a result, he grew to be governed by negative thoughts. As La Bruyere said, "most people spend much of their lives in making the rest of their lives miserable." This is just what Lewis was doing: making his life miserable. All of his energy was being expended on the negative. He was not doing anything constructive to renew his life.

"Lewis, you can choose to go on being miserable. Or you can choose to let God renew your life."

This statement evoked a rather quizzical look. He was not sure how to renew his life.

Our conversation stopped for a while.

The pilot's voice resonated over the speakers asking us to prepare ourselves for landing at the airport in Dayton, Ohio. This was a layover stop for me. This was Lewis's destination.

During the landing approach, Lewis asked if he could lean over to the window to catch a view of the ground below.

With his face to the small window, he said to me, "Dayton, Ohio, the birthplace of aviation." A piece of historical information which only an aviation expert would know.

Both of us disembarked. Standing to the side of the stairs we exchanged addresses while the rest of the commuters filed past us.

Lewis gave me a hug, shook my hand, and casually said, "Keep in touch!"

There was something incomplete in our encounter. Something unresolved.

"Lewis, wait a minute!" I yelled.

Catching up to him through the heatwaves rising from the blacktopped runway, I placed my hand on his shoulder and said we forgot to pray. Far from being startled, his look expressed yearning contentment.

"Lewis, let your mind nest this pleasant thought. God wants to renew your life. You said you have not darkened the doorstep of a church in many years. The church is a treasure house of a precious, peaceful new life for you.

"Go to mass. Let the experience be a confession between God and yourself. Be open and real with him. Then get up from your seat, confidently walk down the aisle of the church, and open your hands to receive the bread of life which was broken for you. Take it to your lips. Like the title of the book you were reading on the plane, take this bread and *Eat to Win*. God wants to renew your life. He will make you a winner."

And then we prayed. Before we left each other I said, "Dayton, Ohio! The birthplace of aviation. You said it yourself. Lewis, let this be the birthplace of your new life today!" I feel the embrace of his strong hug to this day. I knew that peace of mind would come in its own time to him. I saw the unsettled ripples of his life begin to compose themselves into quietness.

"Don't treat your soul carelessly or inconsiderately. It's the most valuable gift God has given to you." With that thought, our encounter became a memory.

Let this day be for you, right where you are, the birthplace of a renewed life. Your soul is the best gift you will ever possess. God's love wants to embrace you and renew you.

FAITH CAN HEAL YOUR LIFE

A *Life* magazine advertisement sponsored by the Phillips 66 oil company, honoring our 1984 Olympic athletes, pictured a diver executing a precision dive, his body knifing the water's surface. Accompanying the ad was this statement:

Everyone starts at the bottom. Real winning comes in not staying there in United States diving; real winning comes when young people learn that it is okay to be afraid; that there is no shame in failing; and as they learn to dazzle the air and knife the water they learn something much more important, that the most soaring triumphs are in simply trying again.

Father Pat, a priest in New York City, had hit bottom. He was telling his story to a gathering of sixty-five people at the weekly Alcoholics Anonymous Meeting in the fellowship hall of the Collegiate Church.

Father Pat is one of the most respected, loving shepherds of hurting New York people. He is also an alcoholic.

Substance abuse destroyed his life, his career, his identity. His alcoholism had been masked in most clever ways as he unfolded the deception of his life in the story of his healing.

At the lowest point in his life, while he lived in the parish rectory, he arrived at the depths of his fraudulent character. Even though he was a priest, he often found himself loitering in front of abandoned buildings where he could hide drinking from his parish community. He spent many hours hustling for change to buy the next drink in local parks.

At night he secluded himself in his bare rectory apartment, which became a jungle of fear, separated from the other floors where staff priests and administrative workers and housekeepers lived.

Although living in a parish rectory, emotionally he felt himself equivalent to those chronic alcoholics who made up about 35 percent of the men living in SROs or "welfare hotels." His personal room, that had once sustained him for private prayer and devotions, was becoming spiritually empty, nothing more than an empty shell, devoid of human dignity, like the cubicles in the crowded homeless residences.

"I had gone as low as preying upon people on the streets or at social functions to secure the support for my own addiction. And while preying on society, I forgot how to pray."

He was emotionally reduced to traumas, cellulitis, and respiratory infections, all frequent complaints of those struggling with the illness of alcoholism. He was failing. If he had a good day, such a small improvement was a triumph for him. Alienating himself more and more from his colleagues, he was disabled by confusion and fear.

Disposing of empty bottles without being discovered by the maintenance staff posed a major problem. In the beginning he deposited them in the shaft incinerator in the rectory until the shatter of bottles in the garbage bins in the basement provoked a number of inquiries and innuendos.

He devised an alternate plan. Accumulating bottles in bags in his closet under piles of old clothing parishioners had brought for flea markets.

Early one morning, dressed in his black pants, shirt, and clerical collar, and with the bags under his arms, he quietly left his home before any of the staff members woke for the day's work.

He drove from New York across the George Washington Bridge to New Jersey where he found a shopping mall. At the edge of the parking lot he found a Salvation Army clothing bin, and there he deposited the clothes for good will and the empty bottles for his own protection.

"If anyone saw a priest depositing clothing in the Salvation Army box, what else would they assume other than the fact that a good deed was being performed by a good priest?" he said, to the laughter of the AA group.

As he stood looking into the dark cavity of the clothing disposal bin, he saw the empty darkness of his own life.

"I had been deceiving God and myself." In this deception he admitted that he had failed. He had hit bottom.

"It was time for me not to stay at the bottom."

Father Pat made an appointment to meet with the bishop of the Archdiocese, in whom he found a loving embrace. This sympathetic Bishop, an endearing friend, a compassionate, caring, and understanding man, placed Father Pat in Guest House, a home in New York City for alcoholic priests. Here faith began to be rekindled. His life healed.

As the *Life* magazine advertisement suggested, he discovered that "it is okay to be afraid and that there is no shame in failing." He was learning something more important, that the "most soaring triumphs are in simply trying again."

Father Pat decided to try again.

For some starting at the bottom is taking the first step into the loving embrace of God, an embrace that has the power to heal. It is the most positive step you can take towards a life that is not self-defeating, a step that can move you beyond disability to good health, emotionally and spiritually.

Once you make that decision to take the first step, you step out onto the greatest foundation upon which to place your life—Jesus Christ. Father Pat started again at the bottom and months later found himself as a whole man celebrating the Eucharist with a congregation who gathered in triumph over their priest's renewed life.

Father Pat was embraced by a loving God and a loving friend, both concerned that he find healing. How discouraged we become when we can not seem to find such support to encourage us.

How often the world seems to provide no charity. It is brusque and unemotional, and people pass us by because they are too busy to care. We think there is no one who cares or who is tender, understanding the suffering of humanity. The impassive, unsympathetic life can also be disarmingly disguised by churches on street corners, with the facades of true goodness, when they often fall short of their mission to be the saintly embodiments of God's all embracing love.

Even if the church has failed, and fallen, it can allow itself to become immersed once again in those baptismal waters, calling itself to a mission of love to hurting people. The church, like Father Pat, cannot afford to stay complacently at the bottom. Winning the kingdom and saving souls does not come from staying where you are. We must continually try again to live by the standards God has set for us and to embrace a world that is struggling to be whole.

Father Pat's renewal did not end at Guest House. It was seen in God's miraculous use of healed and renewed people to help hurting people.

While waiting in an emergency ward of a New York hospital with one of his parishioners, Father Pat heard a nurse ask if there was anyone in the reception room who might be from AA.

Pat approached the nurse's station and offered his assistance in controlling a man who had been admitted in an un-leashed emotional stage of intoxication.

As several doctors and interns worked to sedate the man, Father Pat, who was not wearing the typical priestly garb, began talking with him.

The drunk yelled, "Who are you?"

"I'm a member of AA."

With swinging arms, the man screamed for him to get out of the room.

"Don't give me any of that AA garbage! Get out!"

Before leaving, Father Pat removed a calling card from his wallet and told him, "If you ever need anyone to talk to, here is my card. Call me. I'm willing to listen. My name is Father Pat." He placed his hand on the emergency room doorknob to leave.

The man yelled, "Wait a minute. You're a priest?!"

"Yes," replied Father Pat.

Motioning to him to come closer to his bed, this hopeless looking man, drained of all of life's dignity said, "So am I! I've been living in the Bowery for thirteen years. In the gutters."

Father Pat spent months with this man as a close compan-ion and encourager. Having been at the bottom, he knew of the potential to heal. Pat embraced him with love. Their lives were both embraced by God's faith in them. And Father Pat's loving embrace encouraged this alcoholic to become a resident at Guest House.

Two years later Father Pat sponsored this priest at his installation service, installing him as a healed, renewed child of God. Faith in God's loving embrace has the power to heal your life. Remember you are always a "guest" in God's house. He will always prepare a table for healing before you.

FAITH CAN RESTORE YOUR LIFE

In "Adonais" Shelley said,

> Life, like a dome of many-colored glass,
> Stains the white radiance of eternity,
> Until Death tramples it to fragments.

Sometimes the experiences of life discolor God's intended splendor and creation. Our dreams are smashed to fragments and all our hopes trampled upon. But faith restores us to hope and life for faith provides us with a promise of eternity. The Wisdom of Solomon says that "the souls of the righteous are in the hand of God, and there shall no torment touch them."

As long as you are in that loving embrace of God, held in His hands, nothing can harm you. It is an embrace from which you can never be separated. The Scriptures say, "Nothing can separate us from the love [embrace] of God."

This is the promise that helped restore Ed and Evelyn Troost to faith.

The Troosts, along with their twenty-eight-year-old son Dale, were members of a former church of mine. Dale's wonderful voice helped to fill our church with songs of faith, as each week he faithfully sang in the church choir in this small United Methodist congregation. His ministry of discipleship in the congregation revealed his apparent gifts for ministry and the movement of God within his life. Dale felt the Lord was calling him to ministry and often shared the excitement of the possibility of giving his life to full-time Christian service. Our visions and goals were closely linked. We were brothers in the Spirit.

Ed and Evelyn had another son, Eddie, who died of cancer at age thirty, just a few years before they joined my congregation. They came to my pastoral leadership as they were emerging from grief over the loss of their elder son.

At the same time they were feeling the emotional repercussions of their daughter Tottsie's painful divorce. Ed and Evelyn's lives were filled with pain. Life was fragmented for them, much of its joyous color dulled with despair.

About a year after they became actively involved in our congregational life, the Troosts attended Sunday morning worship with anguish on their faces. At the end of our celebrative hour of praise and joy, they embraced me at the front door with the sad news that a job transfer would be moving them out of state. I would miss their radiant faith and their complete commitment and dedication to our ministry. The departure would create a tremendous void of love within my life.

As they relocated in Michigan, Dale moved on to Colorado where he took up residency with his sister. His stay was to be prematurely short-lived.

Driving home from work one evening, he lost control of his small Datsun and was instantly killed as his car rolled down an embankment. The many-colored dome of God's love above the Troosts seemed to shatter as death trampled it into fragments. In their immense pain, the white radiance of eternity was stained once again.

A few days later I stood in front of Dale's casket, giving witness to the gospel proclamation of new life. Someone once said, "Joys too exquisite to last, and yet more exquisite when past." Much joy had been brought into the Troosts' lives by their son, Dale—a joy too exquisite to last. His death made us all realize more the presence of that joy, a more exquisite splendor because of the painful loss that endears one even more fondly to our hearts. This family was overwhelmed with stress. They were now drifting in a sea of lifelessness. Pain had numbed them. They struggled to keep their lives together. Only faith would restore them.

A year later Ed Troost was visiting in New York, his first visit to my new congregation after Norman Peale had called me to serve in the Collegiate Church.

In the solitude of my office he conveyed to me the inspiring, emotional events of his few days of business in New Jersey and New York.

In Jersey, Ed decided to drive to the home where he had once lived when the whole family were happily together. As he sat in his car, parked in front of this home, he remembered all the family occasions for joy and laughter. He captured special moments when he held the vivid remembrances in still frames in his mind. Evelyn. Eddie. Dale. Tottsie. In grief he wept.

He then drove to the apartment where they lived after their elder son Eddie died, a place of painful reshaping and future promises. The church had once again assumed a vital role in their lives. They were growing in God's loving embrace.

The remembrance, even here, created more moments of crying.

He then went to the Verona United Methodist Church,

where they were members and where I served as their minister. Seated in the solitude of the peaceful sanctuary, Ed glanced up at the choir loft where Dale used to sing, yearning to hear in his heart the music that had become so dissonant with tragedy. His emotions incapacitated him.

Heading for New York, Ed felt unresolved. Rather than having received peace through times of remembrance, his soul was more disturbed.

Exiting on the next ramp of the turnpike, his car made a U-turn and headed back to New Jersey.

Slowly he brought his car to a halt in front of the home where they had lived as a whole family.

"God, thank you for all the wonderful, precious moments that were created and birthed, shared and celebrated here with my family."

At the curb in front of the apartment building he again prayed, "God, help me to remember that even in my time of grief, as I was adjusting to the loss of my son, that here in this home, I grew to rely on You even more. Help me and Evelyn to trust You even more for the restoring of our lives today."

Returning to the small church, he walked down the aisle and knelt at the communion rail.

"God, I can't handle my life alone anymore. I turn my life, my pain, my brokenness, my future over to you."

In surrender of his cares and life to God he felt the power of the Lord around him. He was embraced by the love of God. In that embrace he found the strength, the power of faith, that would make him strong.

Jesus said, "Lo, I am with you always." The original Greek interpretation of this phrase was distorted in its translation. The Greek was more emphatic in its intention:

"Lo, *I,* with you, *am,* always."

The "I AM," God Himself, is always around you, always with you, embracing your life. When you grasp Him and cling to His love with complete trust, God will restore your life.

Remember the secret and promise of being restored,

healed, and renewed. Hold on to the cross. Let Christ live in you. Live in Him. You will discover that Christ is a Christ of power. Grasp this secret. And Christ will place within you all the hope of the glorious things to come. Simply starting again is a triumph. Why not start this day, this moment, in God's loving embrace. Above you once again, you will see the dome of God's splendid love, filled with the "white promises of eternity."

The soul seeks the light in each of us, the deeper feeling of the beauty and joy of living. God will always place above you and within you the light of his love, a love that will make you strong.

CHAPTER 7

Power for Living in God's Embrace

A *New York Times* article featured this disturbing headline on the front page: "Some Elderly Choose Suicide over Lonely, Dependent Life."

Suicide! An increasing statistic among the young and elderly who no longer find meaning in their existence. Overwhelmed by an inability to cope with life's pain, they seek solace through death. Suicide provides a solution to a life of loneliness, confusion, and despair.

There is another alternative even though life may appear futile. If you embrace God's power for living, you can find your life restored to joy and hope.

The article on elderly suicide tells of a housecleaner named Margaret Plahn. When Mrs. Plahn finished her housecleaning work in Eric and Lotte Snyder's apartment, it struck her as strange that Mrs. Snyder kissed her good-bye. She had never done that before. The elderly Snyders, both immigrants from Germany, were going through a difficult time.

The eighty-one-year-old Mr. Snyder, who had been blind for five years, still swam for exercise and tried to remain self-sufficient and independent. His eighty-eight-year-old wife, who had cared for him for many years in their affluent apartment south of San Francisco, had gone almost totally blind too.

An understanding and sympathetic Mrs. Plahn adapted the apartment for the blind couple. She fixed tiny pieces of sandpaper to the stove dials to assist Mrs. Snyder in her daily cooking.

Yet the Snyders continued to feel increasingly helpless. Meals came out wrong. The chicken was raw or the pastry burned. At the end of the week, Mrs. Plahn baked the couple a cake as a weekend treat.

Returning to work on Monday morning, the housekeeper became alarmed when no one answered the doorbell. She entered the apartment with the building superintendent and found a note on a foyer table.

Both Eric and Lotte were seated on their sofa, loving arms around each other, in an embrace of death—an overdose of phenobarbital. The housekeeper's words resonate with sadness: "They gave in just to have peace."

The sad fact today is that people sometimes "give in" in order to find peace rather than embrace the love of God that will give to them a peace the world cannot offer. And so, in giving in to find peace, they fail to grasp the powerful love of God and find peace in its fulfillment.

Not only is our world filled with fragile people. The world itself is fragile. Brittle. Easily broken. Weak. Liable to fail. Easily destroyed. Frail. Delicate.

Fragile people who rely on a fragile world will become fragmented. A fragment is a part broken off, separated. It becomes detached, isolated, incomplete.

A fragile world can never make you whole. Only the love of God, as it embraces you and the world, can make you complete, and offer to the world its only hope. Jesus said, "Do not fear, little flock [fragile people], for it is your Father's good pleasure to give you the kingdom. . . . provide yourselves . . . a treasure in the heavens that does not fail, where no thief approaches nor moth destroys. For where your treasure is, there your heart will be also."[1]

Only God's loving embrace will make you whole.

Let God embrace you, and you will receive life's greatest power for living. This power for living is a gift given by a redemptive, caring God. It is His freely to bestow. Such a love is ours freely to receive. Isolated from that embrace we will be separated from the love of God.

Remember, that "nothing can separate us from the love of God" except our own choice not to embrace His gift of love.

In *Carrying the Fire,* astronaut Michael Collins takes us with him to the moon on *Apollo 11* and provides us with an extraordinary image of our world and its people. Michael Collins says:

> If I could use only one word to describe the earth as seen from the moon, I would ignore both its size and color and search for a more elemental quality, that of *fragility.* The earth appears "fragile," above all else. I don't know why, but it does. As we walk its surface, it seems solid and substantial enough, almost infinite as it extends flatly in all directions. But from space there is no hint of ruggedness to it; smooth as a billiard ball, it seems delicately poised in its circular journey around the sun, and above all it seems fragile. Once this concept of apparent earthly fragility is introduced, one questions whether it is real or imagined, and that leads inexorably to an examination of its surface. There we find things are very fragile indeed. Is the sea water clean enough to pour over your head, or is there a glaze of oil on its surface? Is the sky blue and the cloud white, or are both obscured by yellow-brown air-borne filth? Is the riverbank a delight or an obscenity? The difference between a blue and white planet and a black and barren one is delicate indeed.[2]

We live in a fragile world populated by fragile people entrusted with a planet they have made brittle by misuse of resources.

Today, the delicateness of our planet and of its humanity is emphasized especially by the potential obliteration of our human race and our home called earth by the ever-increasing threat of nuclear war.

On August 6, 1945, President Harry S. Truman shared with the American people a statement about the bombing of Hiroshima. His statement reminds us that we live in a world made fragile, not by the threat of nuclear war, but by the reality that we live in a world that has known such a holocaust.

Its horror is forever embedded in the historical collage of human experience. On that pivotal day of misguided power, Truman said: "Sixteen hours ago an American airplane dropped one bomb on Hiroshima. It is a harnessing of the basic power of the universe. The force from which the sun draws its power has been loosed against those who brought war to the Far East. We have spent two billion dollars on the greatest scientific gamble in history—and won."[3]

Only one truth emanates from this historical statement. The deployment of this annihilating tool was, and is still today, the greatest gamble in history. The human race, embraced by war, can never win. Humanity embraced by God's love will find its mending and wholeness only from that embrace.

The folly of humanity's misuse of such power can only result in the furthering fragility of the world and of humankind's character. A nuclear warhead is not the harnessing of the basic power of the universe.

As people of faith, embraced by God's love, we discover that the greatest power for living comes when the world is harnessed by God's loving embrace. It is this embrace that will heal a broken and fragile people. Today, our world is being threatened by human nature's misuse of power. Our consuming passion reminds us that our hope in life, the only hope for our world, is Jesus Christ.

Without the all embracing love and hope of God, the world and our lives will remain fragile. The earth will be easily destroyed.

Find hope and peace in God's embrace. The greatest power for living is offered by Christ, dwelling within us and giving us a peace the world can never produce for itself.

The incarnation, the atonement, were the greatest harnessing of the basic power of the universe. The omnipotence of God. Unlike the nuclear bomb (our world's greatest gamble), salvation history has provided all humankind with a victory in Christ, life's greatest power for living. Only in that embrace can the world win and you and I survive.

Michael Collins continued his assessment of the earth's fragility by saying:

> I really believe that if the political leaders of the world could see their planet from a distance of 100,000 miles, their outlook could be fundamentally changed. That all-important border would be invisible, that noisy argument suddenly silenced. The tiny globe would continue to turn, serenely ignoring its subdivisions, presenting a unified facade that would cry out for unified understanding, for homogeneous treatment. The earth *must* become as it appears: blue and white, not capitalist or Communist; blue and white, not rich or poor; blue and white, not envious or envied. . . . There is but one earth, tiny and fragile, and one must get 100,000 miles away from it to appreciate fully one's good fortune in living on it.[4]

We cannot all journey into the vastness of the universe to capture astronaut Collins' image of this fragile earth.

All of us can, however, perceive this world, and our lives through God's eyes.

The psalmist was transported to these spiritual heights which gave him power for living:

> O Lord our Lord,
> How excellent *is* Your name in all the earth,
> *You* who set Your glory above the heavens! . . .
> When I consider Your heavens, the work of Your fingers,
> The moon and the stars, which You have ordained,
> What is man, that You are mindful of him . . . ?
> For You have made him a little lower than the angels,
> And You have crowned him with glory and honor.
> You have made him to have dominion over the work
>   of Your hands. . . .[5]

The psalmist caught a vision of God's world and was challenged to be a creative steward of God's gift of power to His children.

We were created to have dominion over the work of God's hands, not destroyers of His work by our hands, or our own lives by our own hands, as did the couple who took their own lives, giving in to find the peace for which their souls longed.

The psalmist maintained God's perspective of life. He lifted his eyes up to the hills, to God. A life lived outside of God's embrace is easily broken, crushed, defeated. It is incomplete.

Yes, our world is fragile, filled with fragile people. God surveys this planet thrown plummeting through our celestial spheres and "looks down from heaven upon the children of men, To see if there are any who understand, who seek God."[6]

In God's embrace, and in our grasp, is converged life's greatest power for living. Isaiah 45:22 says, "Look to Me and be saved." Power for living begins when we look to God for His loving embrace. This world will blend its boundaries into love when it looks to God. Lives will be made whole when they turn to God.

What would have happened if the elderly couple who gave in, who committed suicide to find peace, had given up their lives to be held in God's tender embrace?

In life you do not have to give in to find peace.

Give your life to God, place yourself in His loving embrace, and know both power and peace.

CHAPTER 8

God's Love Never Fails

Asserting my way through the crowded Damascus Gate at the entrance to the walled city of old Jerusalem, I began walking down the street that led to the Garden Tomb, one of the two locations where tradition suggests that Jesus rose from the dead on that glorious Easter morning.

The serenity of the Garden was undergirded by the sacredness of God's holy presence. The Garden and its numerous outdoor chapels, where people could gather for worship and meditation, was lush with the clustered fragrance of lavender and the penetratingly sweet aroma of rosemary.

The garden's solitude was interrupted by whispers of the faithful in prayer and by the sounds of gravel under quietly shuffling feet. With awe I walked these narrow pathways beneath the low spreading branches of olive trees, escorted by the chanting of birds. The sun's rays shimmered through the gently swaying leaves. Many people stood in quiet reflection reading the Bible.

The sun's intense rays shone brilliantly upon the rocks which descended to the open door of the tomb, perfectly spotlighting the stage where God performed His greatest miracle.

Along the path, I smiled at a gardener on bended knees weeding a flower bed. His warm, reciprocating smile welcomed me to this place where truth revealed that God's love never fails.

I was grateful to walk in the very garden where our risen Lord first appeared to Mary. My thoughts humbly turned to prayer to thank God for the one who made this moment possible, a woman who taught me that God's love never fails.

A year ago July I preached at the historic Ocean Grove Auditorium, in Ocean Grove, New Jersey, Methodism's largest camp meeting ground in the United States. Just three months before this speaking engagement, my wife and I had separated. My message reflected my pain and hurt. My tone and delivery possessed an overbearing somberness. My wound and stress were evident to the congregation of several thousand people—especially to one kind, caring, sensitive, and empathetic woman.

Margarite Herr, a former neighbor on the row of cottages where my wife and daughter owned a summer home, invited me to visit her that Sunday afternoon. Reluctantly, I agreed to pay her a visit.

I could not handle a rehashing of my marital crisis, and I intentionally stayed away from anyone's curious interest in the events which led to our separation, even the best-intentioned supporters. I was still in my denial stage and could not handle a confrontational discussion of my deep pain.

But my marital struggle was not a concern of Miss Herr's. Instead, she strengthened my healing process by providing me with a gift of love that would redirect my life on the pathway to renewal.

"You need some spiritual nourishment," she said. "There is a place, only one experience, that can provide that for you. I want you to walk where someone very special in your life, and in mine, walked!"

"Where do you want to go?" I exclaimed, anticipating that the two of us would get up from the rocking chairs on the cottage porch to head in a direction that had the best of my curiosity.

"I don't want to walk anyplace!" she responded.

With that, Margarite handed me an envelope that contained a generous check. At the memo line, located in the bottom left hand corner were written the words, "Holy Lands."

My emotional barometer began to rise instantly! I was seated before a woman whose generosity revealed just how deeply one human being can feel toward another through the gift of love that God places within their hearts.

Margarite explained, "Years ago, one of the most moving and inspiring experiences I had was to walk in the land where our Savior was born, where God touched our lives with the fullness of His love."

I continued to listen to her explain how that touching moment of visiting the Holy Land was a once-in-a-lifetime spiritual experience, the intensity of which she felt could never be duplicated.

"It has been my desire to send others to walk where Jesus walked. I have sent many people on this journey. This is the year for your pilgrimage, to become more deeply acquainted with the Spirit. To walk with God more closely."

With great humility, I received God's never-failing love. It is always present, never withheld. It is freely given, not only through Him, but through those who love Him and love others.

"God always sends us angels when we need the strength and encouragement to pursue living. Long after I am gone, I want you to remember me as one!" Margarite said.

When I descended the rugged approach to the tomb, the overwhelming significance of the moment began pounding within my chest. Approaching the entrance, I poked my head into the damp chamber. Lifting my feet over the tomb entrance, I moved to a corner known as the outer wailing room. Leaning against the wall, I slid down to sit on the floor of the carved-out tomb.

My eyes were fixed upon the spot where our Lord was buried. There were no tourists inside with me.

But I was not alone!

The loving embrace of God was around me.

My companions were truth and hope and love. We were abiding together!

Removing from my pocket a piece of bread from one of the shops along the Via Delarosa in old Jerusalem, I communed with God and with my Savior.

The floodgates of my emotions ripped open!

This was no midlife crisis. Turmoil, uncertainty, and fear were running currents in my life. Life was filled with many unresolved endings. Facing me was a life of many unknowns, and the most ominous unknown was myself!

I was a minister crouched, crying, in Christ's own tomb. And yet I didn't even know what God saw within me, which gave to this tomb all of its explicit significance.

What did He see in me that was valuable and worth saving? At my own hands, through my own choices, my life was in shambles. Could I discover His loving embrace here? Would a growing trust in Him be the gift released by the stone that was once rolled away from the tomb? Would the weight of my own sins be a burden lifted? What freedom would I discover in this garden?

My marriage and my life were in ruin. I failed! I needed to discover the one who never fails.

The dichotomy of my situation was incredible. Here in the center of hope, I was overshadowed by my own sense of hopelessness.

Dietrich Bonhoeffer said,

> The air in which we live is so infected with mistrust that it is almost bringing us to ruin. But wherever we break through the layer of mistrust, we find there the experience of a trust that we had previously not even dreamed of. We have learned to put our lives into the hands of those we trust. Against all the ambiguity in which our acts and lives have had to stand, we have learned to trust unreservedly.

That was it! I needed to put my life into the hands of the one I could trust unreservedly. To allow Him to break through the layer of my own mistrust and find the gift of new life, previously not even dreamed of.

Hurriedly leafing through the onionskin pages of a pocket New Testament, I turned my eyes upon the gospel story.

> Now when the Sabbath was past, Mary Magdalene, Mary *the mother* of James, and Salome bought spices, that they might come and anoint him. Very early in the morning, on the first

day of the week, they came to the tomb when the sun had risen. And they said among themselves, "Who will roll away the stone from the door of the tomb for us?" But when they looked up, they saw that the stone had been rolled away—for it was very large. . . . Mary stood outside by the tomb weeping, and as she wept she stooped down *and looked* into the tomb. And she saw two angels in white sitting, one at the head and the other at the feet, where the body of Jesus had lain.[1]

The angel said: "Do not be alarmed. You seek Jesus of Nazareth, who was crucified. He is risen! He is not here. See the place where they laid Him."[2]

Before me was the place where they had laid him!
    And the angel said to her,

"Woman, why are you weeping?" She said to them, "Because they have taken away my Lord, and I do not know where they have laid Him."

Now when she had said this, she turned around and saw Jesus standing *there,* and did not know that it was Jesus. Jesus said to her, "Woman, why are you weeping? Whom are you seeking?" She, supposing Him to be the gardener, said to Him, "Sir, if You have carried Him away, tell me where You have laid Him, and I will take Him away."

Jesus said to her, "Mary!" She turned and said to Him, "Rabboni!" (which is to say, Teacher).[3]

I was crying!
    For the first time in my life the Scripture was poignantly directed at me: "Why are you crying? He is not here. He is risen!"
    Deciding to trust unreservedly, I turned toward the tomb entrance and stepped out into the garden's brilliant sunlight to place my life in the hands of the One God told me I could trust, the One who would never fail me.
    I decided to walk into the loving embrace of the risen Lord.
    Turning once more to look at the entrance of the tomb before I left the garden, I remembered the tenth chapter of He-

brews. The words reflected what I had just experienced in the tomb of Jesus: "Let us draw near with a true heart in full assurance of faith, having our hearts sprinkled from an evil conscience and our bodies washed with pure water. Let us hold fast the confession of *our* hope without wavering, for He who promised *is* faithful."[4]

God's promise of new life for you and me can be trusted.

What I needed to learn from that moment on was to "hold fast in the confession of [my] hope"!

I would trust that loving embrace of God, by placing my life within His hands.

God would never fail me. Nor will He ever fail you!

With resilient renewal and affirmation I ascended the steps to the garden. The birds were not the only creatures singing their songs of praise. Singing over and over again in my soul were the wonderful words of life!

A short distance from the garden exit, I passed, once again, the gardener on his knees in a flower bed. Our smiles, this time, blessed each other's departure with an unexpressed, yet acknowledged truth.

When his face turned back to the soil where his hands were turning the earth, I paused to watch him, with a stunned awareness coming to my mind.

And Mary, supposing Him to be the gardener said, "Sir, if you know where they have taken my Lord, tell me so that I may go and find him."

Supposing him to be the gardener?

Why would Mary, in turning from the tomb and seeing Jesus, think that this man, who in reality was the risen Lord, was the caretaker of the garden? It may have been for the very same reason that I knew the man whom I had just walked past to be the gardener. Jesus, the risen Lord on that glorious Easter morn, may have been on His knees, with His hands in the richness of earth's warm soil. Mary saw both the gardener and the Lord. They were one and the same.

It was the creation story from Genesis unfolding again before Mary and all of humanity. Through the risen Christ, the never-failing love of God had forgiven us of our sin and created us anew, lifting us into the embrace of His arms and the touch of

His hands, breathing within us that Easter morn the gift of eternal life.

It was God whom Mary saw in the garden!

And she ran to proclaim to all the world God's never-failing love and promise:

> Jesus was both the Risen Lord and the gardener, creating within us clean hearts.
>
> Jesus was both the Risen Lord and the gardener, renewing within us a right spirit.
>
> Jesus was both the Risen Lord and the gardener, calling us to His loving embrace, never to cast us away from His presence.
>
> Jesus was both the Risen Lord and the gardener, creating within the soil of our souls the breath of the Holy Spirit.
>
> Jesus was both the risen Lord and the gardener, God Himself restoring us to the joy of His salvation.
>
> Jesus was both the risen Lord and the gardener, upholding us with the embrace of His loving spirit.

Trust that loving embrace. It will never fail you.

Trust it unreservedly.

Place your life in the hands of the One you can trust to give you new life. Begin an "experience within your life which you had previously not even dreamed of."

CHAPTER 9

The Embrace of Grace

We cannot put off living until we are ready. The most salient characteristic of life is its coerciveness; it is always urgent, "here and now," without any possible postponement. Life is fired at us point blank.

—Ortega y Gasset

Choose life! This is faith's urgent appeal today. The embrace of grace helps each of us, here and now, to confront life which is fired at us point blank with the life that God offers to us through faith. Grace can constrain us as we face the difficulties of life which can break us.

The embrace of grace allows us to face life's problems head on with a loving God who embraces us as we struggle and grow in our pursuit of life's abundant gifts.

It takes courage to confront life's struggles head on and to emerge from the battle whole and complete. The promise of the embrace of grace is that life's hardest experiences always are "walks through valleys." Grace will lead you home.

Faith always thrusts us forward. Christ's words of grace continually pointed people outward as he presented a hope that would become conspicuously available for them. He became light in darkness. He was conspicuously present as light in life's battle. His embracing grace led to eternal life.

The embrace of grace equips you with faith that is "salient." What a mighty word for facing life which is fired at us point blank.

Salient! Resilient faith on the front lines of living. Salient is also known as the part of a battle line, trench, or fort which projects farthest toward the enemy.

Toward the enemy?

How we would rather run from our problems or avoid them completely. Avoid the pain! But we soon discover that life at a deeper level is lived in the middle of struggle. In the center of pain there is growth. We hear it continually: "No pain, no gain." Yet we'd rather run from the enemy—pain—or even the struggle that leads to growth.

The psychologist Gordon Allport states the need to avoid pain clearly when he refers to an infant's need to minimize pain in the development of its personality as a human being:

> The new born infant is almost together a creature of hered-ity, primitive drive and reflex existence. . . . At this point in development the child is largely a creature of segmental ten-sions and pleasure-pain feelings. They are motivated by the need to minimize pain and to maximize pleasure and with these conditions determined by the reduction of visceral, segmental tensions, the child proceeds to develop.[1]

At all costs, we avoid situations that would maximize pain and minimize joy. As we stretch and grow, however, we discover that painful experiences offer new possibilities for growth. Embraceable grace will sustain you through problems. And problems can help you discover a strong, salient personality. With Christ, you can face life head on.

Healing and wholeness will come into your life when you decide not to run from your problems. They come when you begin to confront the problems, head on, here and now. The apostle Paul said, "with Christ in me I have the power to overcome adversity." Grace will always embrace you as you stand on the battle line, within the trench.

This gives us a clearer picture of God as an almighty fortress; Martin Luther called Him a "bulwark never failing." God does not provide us with a hiding place. He provides us with a grace that empowers us in the center of our living. He is not only a light in the darkness, but a deliverer from the darkness. Psalm 18:2 says,

> "The LORD is my rock and my fortress and my deliverer;
> My God, my strength, in whom I will trust;
> . . . my stronghold.

"I'm gripped by pornography," was the confession shared with me by a young man struggling with an obsession to seek cheap thrills in the sleazy, dark corridors of New York's adult X-rated theaters.

For months he had been able to master his dependence upon pornographic literature, yet the insatiable desire for sexual exploitation was beginning to dictate, once again, a preoccupation with lustful thoughts.

Finding himself in the shadows of these theatres, he was overwhelmed by anxiety and guilt. He was a casualty of his inner war with lust. In the obscure anonymity of the theatre, cramped within the cubicles of unlighted booths, he confronted unknown faces intent upon degrading the character of human nature by violating anyone who would acquiesce to their physical abuses.

It was also here that he recognized one face, one person who was not a stranger to him, but One who had tried to befriend him many times. It was this Friend's hope that such a relationship would assist him in choosing life!

"I panicked when I saw this familiar face. Standing along the walls of the concealed corridors, I found myself beside many undistinguishable faces—except for one, a face that I've had a hard time escaping. While standing there I turned to see Him. It was Christ next to me. Looking at me!"

There they stood together before the urgent here and

now! He had always tried to postpone this moment by putting off fully living.

In anguish, this frightened and confused man expressed his conflict between sin and guilt and the yearning to be free of the crippling, recurring escapade.

"Why am I held captive by this?" he asked the recognizable face next to his. "While in the darkness of the theatre," he continued, "I thought it quite unusual to find myself praying, asking Jesus to help me in my weakness. Of all places to pray. I was praying to One who is so pure and clean, sinless and righteous, in a place that was filled only with sin and darkness."

His constricting pain of guilt evoked a fear that prevented him from comprehending the nature of our Lord to become involved in all that separates us from the love of God. He needed healing and cleansing. He needed to discover the liberating love of Christ that could lift him out of the grasp of this sin. He needed to understand that Christ would stand with him in the center of his battle, even in the dark recesses of an X-rated theatre. While life is fired at us point-blank, Christ enables us to stare at it point-blank with *life!*

This young man was being embraced by grace in the center of disgrace. In his confession, he was discovering how God's grace provides us with His healing, forgiving love, unworthy though we may be:

> Lord, I am not worthy, but say the word and
> I shall be healed.

Even in a sunless theatre, where sin destroys the value of our character, grace intervenes.

In the center of this battle was the struggle between the flesh and the Spirit. In the center of one of life's most degrading arenas, the love of God was at work. Staring into the eyes of this familiar face, the young man saw the choice to be made. Those eyes taught him that he could be "strengthened with all might, according to His glorious power. . . . He has delivered us from the power of darkness and translated *us* into the kingdom of the Son of His love, in whom we have redemption."[2]

This is grace that embraces us in life's problems. God's

grace is amazing! We find Him willing to be with us at the center of our sinning:

> Lord, you have examined me and you know me. You know everything I do. From far away you understand all my thoughts. You see me whether I am working or resting; You know all my actions. You are all around me on every side; You protect me with your power. [Salient love]; Where could I go to escape from you? Where could I get away from your presence? If I lay down in the world of the dead, you would be there. If I flew away beyond the east or lived in the farthest place in the west, you would be there to lead me; you would be there to help me. I could ask the darkness to hide me or the light around me to turn into night, but even the darkness is not dark for you, and the night is as bright as the day. Darkness and light are the same to you. Examine me, O God, and know my mind; test me, and discover my thoughts. Find out if there is any evil in me and guide me in the everlasting way.[3]

All of us have a past in which there is darkness. We sin and fall short of the love of God. What this young man discovered in the dark niches of an X-rated theatre was the presence of the Light of Christ, a God who is willing to descend even to the depths of his own sinning and embrace him with grace.

His conscience, his soul, was being held in the tension of the choices he needed to confront. It was no longer a time for postponing the choice. He could not put off living until he was ready. God was examining him, his thoughts, his choices. He began praying to God to help him decide to choose God's grace and be healed. If he chose the darkness, he never would know wholeness. In the theatre, he and the Lord embraced.

Matthew Linn said, "Healing comes not by discovering the skeleton in the closet, but by discovering Christ in the closet and putting Him on."[4] When you begin to allow yourself to be embraced by this grace, you will begin to grow and heal.

Life is fired at us point-blank. This life is often deceptive in the choices it provides.

In Irwin Shaw's book *Rich Man, Poor Man,* one of the main characters named Dave tells of the power of evil to mask itself in its attempt to entrap the human spirit. The book says,

> A man has to be careful with his numbered days on earth. There is a conspiracy to chain every living child of man to an iron post, in a black pit, and you mustn't be fooled because they paint it all the bright colors of the rainbow and pull all sorts of devilish tricks to make you think that it isn't a pit, it isn't a post, it isn't a chain, but a rainbow.

The power of evil cleverly masks its attempts to win us away from God's will for our lives.

The interceding love of God's grace will encourage us and guide us in making right choices with our lives. Christ's grace will empower us, heal us, and guide us as we find ourselves on the battle line, in the trench of darkness, facing the enemy. When we are in the center of our problems, it is then that we discover God working for His will in our lives.

One of our hymns of faith tells of God's ability to guide us through this life as we commit ourselves to His will:

> O let me feel Thee near me!
> The world is ever near;
> I see the sights that dazzle,
> The tempting sounds I hear;
> My foes are ever near me,
> Around me and within;
> But, Jesus, draw Thou nearer,
> And shield my soul from sin.

A young man caught in the web of the "sights that dazzle!" discovered it to be a pit, a post, a chain, a sin. But he also found Christ in that pit and began to understand the power of His grace that embraces and heals. In an X-rated theatre one person felt the healing embrace of God's love for him. Ezekiel 36:25 says, "Then I will sprinkle clean water on you, and you shall be clean . . . from all your filthiness." This is God's promise. His grace will embrace you, "here and now." It comes without delay. It knows no postponement, except our unwillingness to make an appointment with it. God will use your pain and your problem so that you can grow through grace.

The important thing for us is to learn from our mistakes and to know that we can be healed by grace. We need not allow our mistakes or our sins to be occasions and reminders of guilt.

They can be channels of grace, simply because God works in and through these experiences.

The gift of grace is misused, however, when we do not learn from our failings and our weaknesses and continually backslide into them rather than grow into the One who will heal us of our past. To choose to love Christ more and let His grace and love move through us is critical in our pathway to healing. Matthew Linn says,

> Healing is not the lifting of a foot that never moved or the lifting of a depression of ten years, but the lifting of our minds and hearts to God. We are not healed unless we love Christ more and he loves more through us.[5]

The healing power of grace shows us the right way to live. It provides us with the choice. As a result, grace compels us and requires us to choose life, to choose here and now the right way to live.

I first understood grace in nontheological terms during my rebellious teenage years. Grace was demonstrated in the interplay between parental authority and my emerging independence and denial of any parental control or authority in my life.

Our family dinner was served daily, with punctuality, at 5:30 P.M. Sharp! Dad, who worked across the street from our home, arrived home each evening to the dinner Mom prepared. We were all expected to be at the table by 5:30 for this time of fellowship. I was the only one who broke this routine.

Often I stayed out after the 5:30 dinner call. Preoccupied with neighborhood friends one night, I finally pushed the curfew to its limit: 7:00 P.M. Then I was faced with the inevitable: returning home.

Quietly, I ascended the three flights of stairs, the wooden steps creaking under my lightly placed feet. Standing on the third-floor landing, I peered through the kitchen window. The room was now dimly lit by a night light above the stove. Dishes were air drying in the dish rack, covered by a neatly placed towel. Through the corridor of our home, the blue cast of the television set in the living room was a startling indication that my family was settled down for the evening, except for their seething anger over my tardiness.

Even though a gentle hand turned the doorknob discreetly to open the door, the silence was pierced by a loud, *"Get yourself in here!"* I had no choice. There was no postponing this one. My Dad's voice confronted me with the urgent "here and now," which was being fired at me point-blank.

Cowering, I made my way to the living room, regretting my disobedience and my soon-to-be pronounced punishment. *"You're grounded for a week!"*

Yet during this same encounter I discovered the embracing love of grace. For as I made my way through the kitchen, I glanced down at the stove. A delectable aroma came from the oven. I opened it. There under the glitter of aluminum foil was my supper, an evening meal, kept warm for one irresponsible, rebellious teenager.

While I deserved to be disciplined for my actions, I discovered grace in a meal that was fully prepared, kept warm, and placed on the table before me. Despite my doing wrong, my meal was not denied me.

The power of grace seen in an oven upon my late arrival home is an experience I recall each time I celebrate the Lord's Supper. All of us come to the Lord's table with our accumulated sins, our rebellious natures, which have offended God. Rightfully, we receive His kind and sometimes harsh reprimands.

But God never withholds the Bread of Life from us. For His grace always is an invitation to come to the table of fellowship with Him, to be embraced by Him. His grace always restores us to wholeness. In the breaking of bread we are redeemed by a grace that heals and forgives our sins.

God always allows us to come home. His grace gives the strength to overcome the old temptations. Grace reminds us that "If we confess our sins, He is faithful and just to forgive us our sins and to cleanse us from all unrighteousness."[6]

My own divorce has taught me once more the painful lesson that life's harsh realities are often fired at us point-blank. Through it I have faced one of my most difficult problems head on. The wounds from being on the front line have been deep; the trench has been dark; the pain of leaving home, intense. The problems of my own life have introduced me to faith that is "salient."

Behind the dim unknown, stands God. With you. With

me. He is our fortress, pointing us towards life, embracing us with grace, standing with us in battle, healing us when we are wounded, lifting us when we have fallen, forgiving us when we have sinned. Here and now, without postponement, choose life! Grace always does lead home—to the loving embrace of God's grace.

CHAPTER 10

Faith Makes You Confident

In English the Olympic Games motto reads: "Swifter, higher, stronger."

Similarly, the Bible also has an Olympic text that encourages us to possess a faith that makes us confident:

> But those who wait on the LORD
> Shall renew *their* strength.
> They shall mount up with wings like eagles,
> They shall run and not be weary,
> They shall walk and not faint.[1]

How do we achieve this soaring confident faith? How do we make it the necessary plus quality within our lives that will assist us in being swifter in our motivation, to soar higher when the problems and difficulties of life weigh us down, and to become stronger and more confident when our physical, emotional, and spiritual energies become depleted?

All of us want a "swifter, higher, stronger" life. Faith can make it possible.

Joseph Newton claims that:

> We cannot tell what may happen to us in the strange medley of life. But we can decide what happens in us. How we can take

125

it. What we can do with it and that is what really counts in the end. How to take the raw stuff of life and make a thing of worth and beauty. That is the test of living. Life is an adventure of faith if we are to be victors over it. Not victims of it. Faith in God above us. Faith in the little infinite soul within us. Faith in life and in our fellow souls. Without a faith—the *plus quality*—we cannot really live.

Faith can make you confident. There is no real power for living without the dynamic plus quality of life: Faith! Faith is power for living, life's greatest power for living. And it is the embrace of God's love that helps us to choose this faith that will allow us to soar higher toward our goals, to run more swiftly toward embracing this loving God, and to become stronger in meeting life.

God does not want us to stay at the bottom. With the plus quality of faith we continually learn that we can soar to new triumphs simply by trying again. God's loving embrace and forgiveness allow us to try again. One mistake does not close off our future. The loss of a job does not brand us as unemployable. The breakup of a marriage does not dismiss us as unlovable.

The plus quality of faith makes us triumphant. We possess the power to overcome any obstacle. We cannot tell what may happen to us, but we can decide how we face life and find worth and purpose in all of its experiences.

Faith is the plus quality that offers to us the real power for living. In *The American Crisis* Thomas Paine said, "These are times that try men's souls. . . . we have this consolation with us, that the harder the conflict, the more glorious the triumph. What we obtain too cheap, we esteem too lightly."

While he was speaking about the American colonies, his words poignantly speak of the liberation of our lives, the glory that comes from having survived the conflict.

God embraces you with the power of faith that revitalizes weary hearts. Faith is the substance that provides us with strength in distress and hope in despair. Faith promises us that life can be renewed. The apostle Paul said,

We are hard pressed on every side, yet not crushed; *we are* perplexed, but not in despair; persecuted, but not forsaken;

struck down, but not destroyed—always carrying about in the body the dying of the Lord Jesus, that the life of Jesus also may be manifested in our body. . . . Therefore we do not lose heart. Even though our outward man is perishing, yet the inward *man* is being renewed day by day.[2]

The plus quality of faith fortifies you with an ability to handle life. Embrace this faith, this plus quality, and you will go through life swifter, higher, and stronger.

Take the plus quality of faith out of your life and look what becomes evident in this rewritten verse from 2 Corinthians minus the plus quality of faith:

We are afflicted in every way and crushed. Perplexed and driven to despair; persecuted and forsaken; struck down and destroyed. We lose heart and while our outer nature is wasting away, our inner nature is deteriorating also.

Such is the quality of life without the plus quality of faith embracing us in God's love. We do not have to lose heart. We can be confident that the embraceable love of faith can strengthen our hearts if we open ourselves to faith and receive God's love.

It had been several years since I had received a letter from a college friend, so when one arrived from Kathy, I thought it came bearing good news, catching up on overdue correspondence. Tearing the edge of the envelope, however, I slowly removed a letter that was to be one of the saddest communications I have ever received. And yet in its tragedy it spoke of a powerful faith, resilient spirits, two lives sustained by the loving embrace of God.

Dear Ron,

On the evening of June 15, 1981, I went out our back door to find our precious little Seth (two years and two months) had drowned in our swimming pool, and efforts to revive him failed. Later we were informed that a blow to the head due to loss of balance in child's play probably was the cause of death.

In our grief and pain it would be easy to place blame on ourselves or God, but we knew this was not an act of God.

For the Bible teaches that "the thief comes only to steal and kill and destroy; I come that they might have life, and have it more abundantly." Perhaps this life was stolen to shatter our faith, but we will not allow the devil this victory!

Every evening when I put Seth to bed, it was our ritual before prayer to tell him how very much his mommy and daddy loved him and that Jesus loved him too. My own prayers often included, "Thank you, God, for this life on loan." Seth Emmanuel Thomas was dedicated to the Lord from birth, and from the little songs he sang, I know that he knew Jesus perhaps even better than his parents. Seth's middle name, Emmanuel means "God with us." And he truly was even though for a very short while.

Jesus said, "Suffer the little children to come unto me and hinder them not, for to such belongs the kingdom of God. Truly I say to you, whoever does not receive the kingdom of God like one of these shall not enter in." We know Seth is loved and cared for by our Lord.

To the honor and glory of our Lord!
Kathy and Jud

How could such young parents, whose dreams for their lives and for their precious Seth were shattered, find strength, not only to survive their child's tragic death, but also to find meaning and purpose at the depth of their pain? What enabled them to be a citadel of unshakable faith?

What allowed them to continue to be swift, to soar, to be strong?

They were strengthened by the plus quality that gave them a faith during the times that were trying their souls.

Undergirded by faith, embraced by God's love, they received God's personal messenger of strength. They were strengthened by the Holy Spirit sent by God to embrace them and uphold them with great comfort.

Jesus knew of a greater comforter than Himself that would increase faith within us to make us confident. When He was faced with death, God sent to Him a sustaining gift.

That desolate night in the garden, in agonizing prayer, when the disciples fell asleep, Jesus discovered that God was with Him. It is here that we gain a glimpse of the weakness of our

Lord and our ability to slacken our reliance on faith when we are in the center of deep pain and uncertainty. We see Him not only as the Lord of strength, power, and courage, but much like ourselves when confronted with the burdens of life.

He needs a sustaining courage in the face of defeat, a ray of hope in the dismal realities of life. Here is the common ground of weakness between Christ and ourselves. He is weighed down, no longer able to be swift, to soar, to be strong. He is broken.

At this moment, in complete weakness and in complete submission to God, relying on His loving embrace alone, we discover God's desire to uphold us, guide us, and lead us through rocky pathways.

God even sent Jesus an angel to strengthen Him.

Astonishing!

Jesus needed an angel. This man who made multitudes whole, who performed miracles, who was a motivator of faith that could move mountains, who proclaimed that all who believed in Him would possess power for living; this man endowed with God's own power, needed a power, strength, a resource other than Himself.

He needed God's loving embrace. And he received it through an angel whom God sent to embrace Him, to strengthen Him. In weakness He received strength from God, a strength rendering Him capable of bearing a cross.

The same strength made Kathy and Jud capable of bearing the death of their son.

Jesus' whole life was surrounded by the power of the Spirit that would give Him a faith to make Him confident. He was conceived in Mary by the power and strength of the Holy Spirit. In life's temptations, He depended on angels to strengthen Him. In the garden before His death, once again He is surrounded by these messengers of strength. At his dying, He commits Himself to that Spirit of God's strength and loving embrace. "Into Your hands I commend my Spirit," Jesus said. Into God's loving embrace. Jesus knew he would find confidence there.

Both Kathy and Jud, with the loss of their child, and Jesus, in His death, turned their weakened lives over to God's loving embrace, an embrace that filled them with the plus quality of life—faith!

At this time of relinquishing self to God's tender care they were able to discern the invincible presence of God, a God who never would leave them comfortless.

Life tries us and tests us.

Reginald was a high school classmate of mine. It had been many years since I saw him. He was told by many people that he would not amount to anything. In the ghettos of Newark, such unsupportive attitudes could have resulted in an unproductive life, in underachievement, if Reg had succumbed to the world's opinion of himself. But he did not.

I remember having my own dreams challenged on the vocational aptitude tests. My high school results placed me in the category of professional opportunities that excluded ministry.

It was at this point that I knew that the Holy Spirit's ability to "call one to the ministry," did not exist through any test results. On the opposite page from my qualifying choices, standing out in blaring letters was the word *ministry*. Committed to that dream and calling, I checked the box for ministry regardless of my tabulated score.

A few weeks later my test evaluator, reviewing my results, called me into his office, explaining to me my apparent error in vocational choice and my misunderstanding of the test results.

I told him it was a selection intentionally made. "I want to be a minister," I said.

He informed me that I did not "rate" in that category and that my test results would be invalid if I did not change my selection.

For my counselor I changed it.

But I left his office knowing my intention to pursue a calling to the ministry, confident this was what I wanted to do and what God was calling me to do.

Fourteen years later, when my wife was in the hospital recuperating from a miscarriage, I came into her room while the resident intern was examining her.

He looked familiar. Glancing at his name tag I made the connection through his name. "Reg Jenkins!" I said. "Art's High School in Newark!"

He associated his patient's last name with mine and said, "Ron Cadmus!"

We shook hands. Fourteen years later he was a medical doctor and I an ordained minister. He was told he would not amount to anything. Here he stood before me a young doctor.

I was an ordained minister.

Reginald Jenkins, an M.D. in a prestigious hospital. Ron Cadmus, one of the ministers of the Collegiate Churches of New York City.

When we stand strong in the Lord and are confident in the power of His might, we have a partner who will enable us to pursue and fulfill our dreams and whose design for our lives will embrace us and lead us to that fulfillment.

Life might threaten you with obstacles. Have confidence in yourself—and in Him, the author and finisher of faith. This faith will make you confident.

God knows "the you that could be!"

In *The You That Could Be,* Fitzhugh Dodson gives an uninhibited definition of confidence:

> You are full of zest and enthusiasm for life. You are spontaneous and outgoing. You have no fears of trying new things. You are not worried about what others think of you. You are able to express the full range of all your feelings: joy, excitement, love, fear, sadness and anger. You have a deep capacity for intimacy and closeness and you are able to love and be loved in return. You have an enormous curiosity about the world and a powerful drive to learn all you can about it. Your self-confidence is solid and secure. You are not anxious or depressed; instead you have a hearty, rollicking enjoyment of life.[3]

Does that sound like you? Is your self-confidence solid and secure?

Is it?

You are not anxious or depressed! You are motivated to be swifter, higher, stronger! Are you really?

Or are you just the opposite? Cast down? Discouraged? Frightened of life? Anxious? Distressed? Worried?

Dr. Dodson surprises us by stating that this definition of

enthusiasm for life is a description of a toddler, a mere child whose confidence is solid and secure.

In such a definition we recapture the potential of Christ's intent behind His statement, "Unless we become like children we cannot enter the kingdom of God." Unless we have solid, secure, self-confident attitudes about life, ourselves, others, and God, we will never know the joy of achieving all the wonderful and great experiences that God has provided for us in our life-time.

You have a life that is filled with unlimited possibilities. But how do you begin to believe and perceive that within you lie the measureless resources of God to do His creative work to make you confident, that you possess power for living, that you are embraced by His love that gives you a faith that will make your life bright with many opportunities?

LOVING GOD WILL GIVE YOU CONFIDENCE

We know that all things work together for good to those who love God, to those who are the called according to *His* purpose. . . . whom He predestined, these He also called; whom He called, these He also justified; and whom He justified, these He also glorified.[4]

This affirmation is necessary for you to begin an exciting life-fulfilling partnership and adventure with God. When we place our life in His will and keeping, we will gain a faith that will make us confident.

Only under this affirmation can we do all things through Christ who strengthens us. We are given power for living by living in the powerful embrace of God's love. Anything short of this absolute faith will result in unfulfilled living.

Without faith it is possible to lack confidence within yourself. It is difficult to comprehend, then, why people, with faith, still often lack confidence in themselves. Why?

As I realistically look at life I am truthfully aware that I am qualified to do some things because of special talents and that I had best leave some other things alone. Math, for instance was one of my worst subjects. In fact, I still count on my fingers to balance a checkbook. Perhaps this is a reason why I seem never to be able to balance monthly statements.

Just give yourself the exercise of looking in the classified section of the newspaper, and you will clearly define where you have qualifications and where you lack them. For instance:

> "Wanted: *Nuclear Radiation Analyst*. Master's degree or higher in nuclear engineering and detailed working knowledge of neutron and proton transport codes for one, two, and three dimensional geometries with a good working knowledge of the cross-section libraries is required. Work experience with nuclear reactors in industry or at national laboratories or direct experience in controlled thermonuclear research is desirable. The successful candidate will have at least four years experience."

Unequivocally, such a job description disqualifies me. First of all, I have no idea what the job description means. For that matter, I could not tell you what a nuclear radiation analyst is or does.

But what happens when people with degrees in nuclear radiation lack the confidence that they have the potential to qualify for such a position? Their fears and lack of faith in themselves prevent them from applying for the position with the belief that they just might be successful in meeting all the requirements and thus securing the job. A plus quality is lacking within their minds—faith in themselves.

No matter how qualified we might be, a lack of confidence will immobilize us with fear. We will then never be swift in going after the position, never soar to attain our goals, never be strengthened in the courage that we can achieve life's successes.

But a sense of confidence, a deep faith in God, can do far more within us than we ever thought or imagined.

While standing at a McDonald's counter waiting for my order, I glanced over to an employment opportunity poster. Under the great golden arches it said: "Golden Opportunity! Help wanted: No experience necessary. Just an enthusiastic and inspired spirit."

Now, that job was for me. I knew I could be hired for it

on the spot. I was certain I was an enthusiastic person with an inspired personality. I was confident of that!

Christ has a golden opportunity for you and your life under the arch of His loving embrace. The only requirement is that you are filled with an enthusiastic, spirit-filled faith.

God works for good with those who love Him with such an attitude of faith in everything they do. He will enable you to develop your fullest potential. If you lack the confidence, you will never achieve even that for which you are qualified.

FAITH WILL MAKE YOU CONFIDENT IN YOURSELF

If you do not believe in yourself, how do you expect God to work through you?

Catherine and David Mitchell were a couple who believed in themselves.

They were confident about their life and work. They lived on Main Street in Point Reyes Station in California. Main Street is one block long. A shoe repair shop and the local newspaper, *The Point Reyes Light,* a sixteen-page weekly distributed to 2,700 people, occupy one building on this street.

Catherine and David owned the newspaper and employed one full-time reporter.

There was great confusion in this town because television cameras and reporters had arrived to film Catherine and David and their small newspaper. They had just won a Pulitzer prize over the national major newspapers for their coverage of Synonon, a controversial drug rehabilitation center under investigation by the state's attorney.

A sixteen-page weekly newspaper, *The Point Reyes Light,* became the shining light of the community and of the journalistic world—all because a young couple believed in themselves and were fully committed to their goals and dreams. Their confidence was solid and secure, and they did the best they could with their small local newspaper. As a result, they knew the joy of success and fulfillment. Their confidence taught them the joy of soaring to greater heights.

They started at the bottom with a small business. But

they were not willing to stay there. This young couple discovered that great triumphs come from simply trying again and again.

Like Kathy and Jud, they possessed the plus quality of faith that made them persevere and endure. Faith qualified them to survive, to grow, to be strengthened, and to soar above all of life's difficulties.

Faith will give you a positive attitude about yourself. Jean, a mentally impaired teenager of one of my former youth groups, brought one of her own culinary creations to the senior high bake sale. It certainly was not a culinary delight. It looked far from appetizing.

We were rather embarrassed to place it among all the other cakes on the table. Hesitatingly we did, asking the same three dollars for it as we asked for all the other baked goods.

One by one the cakes were purchased. As each cake was removed, Jean stood nearby pushing her cake slowly toward the center of the table, thinking its position on the table would call attention to it.

As I suspected, Jean's cake was the last remaining baked item. "Mr. Cadmus, no one bought my cake," she cried.

How do we turn this into a positive situation? I wondered. How could we make Jean feel confident about what she had created by her own hands? We still had some coffee left so I thought we could run a special. Push the last cake along with coffee.

"Jean, run to the kitchen and get a knife." She quickly returned, and I proceeded to cut the cake, four rows across, four rows down.

Sixteen slices at twenty-five cents a slice. One by one they began to disappear until only crumbs were left on the plate. Jean held an empty cake plate in one hand, a broad smile on her face, and sixteen quarters in her other hand.

Four dollars!

Her cake pulled a dollar more than any other cake! That unappealing, culinary misfortune claimed the highest price.

God has the ability to take life's heartaches, impossible situations, bitterly tragic moments, and show us the plus quality of faith that provides all people with confidence and hope.

He gives us the ability to take a negative situation and turn it into a wonderful experience for growth. This can happen if we become empowered by the loving embrace of God, in it finding the quality of faith that will give us confidence for living. Any way we cut it!

And, like Jean, be filled with all that will encourage you to find a hope that will make you swift, allow you to soar, and increase your strength.

Remember, triumphs come from simply trying again. God will always provide you with new opportunities to discover His abundant life. Let His embrace carry you to greater heights and fill you with life's plus quality—faith!

CHAPTER 11

The Embraceable Look of Love

*I*f looks could kill . . ."
This common phrase is used often to convey our attitudes and perceptions about outward appearance. Perhaps you have used this statement or have even suffered its cruel criticism.

Looks! Appearances! We can feel warmly embraced by them or kept at a distance through their cold indifference or hateful glare.

Another frequently used expression to impart reactions to negative facial expressions is, "If you smiled, you'd crack your face!" Some looks contain daggers. Other expressions can convey what Byron claimed: "Soft eyes looked love to eyes that spake again."

To look down on! Still another phrase that conveys inferiority. It suggests that one is regarded with contempt, despised.

Or simply to look on! To regard, to esteem, to consider.

To look! To try to see or find something. I like the definition from Webster: to bring to a certain condition by looking.

"Jesus, looking at him, loved him."[1] Jesus' embraceable look of love, God's love, is intended to help direct an individual to discover the richest blessings of the kingdom of God. Christ's look of love invites one to discover the joy of eternal life by following Him.

As the story in Mark conveys, a man ran up to Jesus, fell on his knees and said, "Good teacher, what shall I do that I may inherit eternal life?" Jesus said, "You know the commandments: 'Do not commit adultery,' 'Do not murder,' 'Do not steal,' 'Do not bear false witness,' 'Do not defraud,' 'Honor your father and your mother.'"

"Teacher," the man declared, "all these I have observed from my youth."

"*Jesus, looking at him, loved him. . . .* 'One thing you lack: Go your way, sell whatever you have and give to the poor, and you will have treasure in heaven; and come, take up the cross, and follow Me.'"

The man's face fell. His look turned away from Jesus. He went away sad because he had great wealth.[2]

Jesus was trying to bring this man to a certain condition and position in life. Through His look, He did more than embrace this man with abundant life. He simply stated how he could find it. "Follow Me!"

But the man's face fell. The embraceable look of love was separated. The man could not tell Jesus how he felt about Him, nor was he willing to respond to the promise that Jesus was readily providing him. By choice he looked away from Jesus. In walking away from Jesus, he discovered sadness.

Jesus Christ wants you to walk towards Life! By following Him! He is the provider of everything we need. Yet in the one who asked Jesus how to inherit eternal life and the one to whom the answer was given reflects our frequent inability to convey to God, through the expression of our feelings, our love for Him.

Jesus looked on him and loved him. But the man's eyes fell away. He went away sad.

Jesus' look always embraces us with love. God perceives goodness in all people. His embraceable look of love provides us with the way to a fulfilled life. The man in the story from Mark simply could not return that look. And thus the potential of life's greatest love affair was denied.

The important affirmation to remember, however, is that while we might take our eyes off God, Jesus will always look upon us with that embraceable look of love. The man's eyes fell *away* from Jesus. Jesus' eyes fell *upon* him! If you ever turn from

Him or have turned from Him, you will discover that He will never leave you out of His sight.

This is how one man learned to love the Lord. He said: "One morning as I was going to work, I was thinking of the words, 'Simon, son of Jonas, lovest thou me?' and wished with all my heart that I could answer them as Peter did. I felt sad that I could not. Then this thought came to me. 'Well, if I cannot say so much as Peter, perhaps I could turn it around a little and find something easier.'

"So I began to think there was one thing I could not say. I could not say, 'Lord, Thou knowest that I *do not* love Thee.' And I found some comfort in that. At last, I grew bold enough to look up and say, 'Lord, Thou knowest that I want to love Thee.' Then I began to think of His great love for me. I thought of His life, of His words, of His cross, and almost before I knew what I was doing, I looked up and said, 'Thou knowest that I do love Thee.'

"And at that moment the consciousness of forgiveness and a new life came into my heart."

These words from Tom Olson teach us two things: first, that it is difficult to express our feelings, to tell others that we love them; secondly, that we need to be bold to look up into the Lord's eyes and simply say, "I love you." When you think of our Lord's great love for us, (Looking upon us He loved us!) we cannot hold our feelings of love for Him captive within.

I believe that as the man's eyes fell away from Jesus and as he walked away from the giver of the treasure he sought, Jesus continued to watch him walk away with that embraceable look of love. The Lord would continue to seek him until that day he chose for himself to "follow Him."

An old Jewish legend confirms that God's nature is to seek those who turn from Him.

According to this legend, when God was about to create man, He took into His counsel the angels that stood about his throne.

"Create him not," said the angel of Justice, "for if Thou dost he will commit all kinds of wickedness against his fellow men; he will be hard and cruel and dishonest and unrighteous."

"Create him not," said the angel of Truth, "for he will be false and deceitful to his brother-man, and even to Thee."

"Create him not," said the angel of Holiness, "he will follow that which is impure in Thy sight, and dishonor Thee to thy face."

Then stepped forward the angel of Mercy (God's best beloved) and said: "Create him, our heavenly Father, for when he sins and turns from the path of right and truth and holiness, I will take him tenderly by the hand and speak loving words to him and then lead him back to Thee."

God will not give up on His desire to embrace you with His love. His embraceable look will forever seek to lead you home to Him.

In the candlelit atmosphere of the restaurant, her face reflected the subtle warmth of candle glow on her cheekbones. Her eyes radiated the flickering light caught in the moisture of her glance. It was the first time I had seen this starlight splendor in her eyes, which made watching her appearance a pleasing experience.

The wrinkles around her eyes began to accentuate her maturity, not so much from years of growing wise but from the years of strain and stress in her personal life. They etched the character of life, as life brushed the strokes of struggle and strength within her soul. This appearance captured both a ruddy fortitude and deep serene confidence.

Candle glow at a formal dinner table allowed me to see the character and detail of this woman's beautiful face.

I was falling in love with her. From across the table, separated only by the candle and a rose in a silver bud vase, our hearts were fusing.

Looking upon her, I loved her. How strange. Meeting each other for the first time and falling in love. Our first dinner alone. It was long overdue. It was here that we began to discover, to love, and to support one another. My deepest feelings cascaded from my heart. I told her how I felt about her.

The difference in our ages was of no concern to me. She was forty-one. I was thirty-eight. For many years, I had watched her from a distance, not really knowing her, yet knowing I loved her.

She never knew my feelings. The reason? Not so much that I was unable to convey those feelings. I never took the time to speak them.

The food that was to strengthen us at this meal would come from no menu or from the specialty of the house. It would come from our open, vulnerable hearts, which would nourish us for the journey of the days and even life ahead.

We looked at each other with an embraceable look of love.

Looking on her, I loved her. Inwardly and quietly I thanked God for this wonderful gift at my table.

She was my sister, Joyce. Brother and sister recognized the unique gift of each other after nearly forty years.

When I was fifteen, Joyce was married at eighteen. Our lives were worlds apart. Different interests separated us. Contrasting values never included our sibling relationship. She circulated among friends whom I never knew, and mine were just as anonymous to her. There was a strong loss when she bade our family good-bye.

If we ever did anything well together, it was dancing. We were both good on our feet, always gaining the glances and attention of the crowd.

Her last night in our home, I danced with her to a slow ballad by Connie Francis: "Where the Boys Are, Someone Waits for Me." Our dancing embrace was a loving embrace, the last to be shared for many years.

After Joyce married, we did not see her often. Then my graduation from Arts High School in Newark and enrollment at West Virginia Wesleyan College, followed by four years of seminary, completely separated us through our young adult years.

My first church appointment to a small Methodist congregation placed me in a town only a few miles from her home. But still, for seven years, we rarely saw each other—not because we had any grievance against each other but simply because we never made the effort. Our lives had taken different paths.

At forty-one and thirty-eight, I was sitting at a table with a woman who had just a few months before gone through a tragic divorce after years of unfulfilling relationship. I was now another statistic of marriage erosion. A petition for divorce, initiated by my wife, resulted in my own broken life.

As we shared our pain and hurt, our warmth and affection, the tight bud of our lives began to unfold like the rosebud on the table. It was an evening of intimate thoughts.

I was in crisis and hurting. I began sharing with my sister my faults, the complex facets of my life that caused the collapse of my marriage and the uncertainty about myself. Her embraceable look of love permitted me to share my worst sins.

In tears I unburdened my heart, as her piercing eyes glanced through mine. Was she examining me with an appraising, scrutinizing eye? No. I was able to sense the embraceable look of her love and to resort to it with confidence and the expectation of receiving acceptance and love.

After I unraveled the threads of life's experiences which had bound me in years of guilt, in quiet confidence she returned the fork and knife to the side of her dish.

Sliding her hand across the table, placing it gently and reassuringly upon mine, she gave a simple yet powerful response to all that I confessed.

"Nothing you have told me, or could tell me, would change my feelings for you. Your past is past! To the worst you've told me, I say, 'I love you still.'

"Look at me," she said.

It was an embraceable look of love.

"And Jesus, looking on him, loved him."

My sister, looking on me, loved me. And I loved her.

In each other's embraceable look, we were able to take a new look at each other and ourselves.

"You shared your faults and sins with me. Do you want to know mine?" Without allowing a response, she proceeded to remove the veneer of her outward disguises. We had touched the essence of our reality.

"You were always seen as the perfect one," she said. "High school honor society. Outstanding student of the City of Newark school system at your graduation. Successfully completing college. And then the epitome of perfection—ordination and the ministry. Yours was always an upright, upstanding life of integrity and achievement.

"There was no way that I could match it or live up to you." With tears of release she hugged me saying, "I am so glad to know that you are not perfect." And that was simply OK! In one evening we had discovered each other to be acceptable and forgivable.

I met a woman for the first time that day. My sister. We found each other in the embraceable look of love. We had looked on each other. And whom we saw, we loved.

In the same way, as we confess our lives before Jesus Christ, we discover a Friend who looks upon us and loves us. He knows we are not perfect and loves us still. When we look to Him we find the embraceable look of love.

But why do we wait so long to reveal to Him and to share with those who are closest to us, our love and our lives? Why do family members remain so passively distant, relating only on the surface of existence, never touching the soul and heart? What creates the difficulty in being able to look at each other through the embraceable look of love, that can nurture us to wholeness and fulfillment, acceptance and forgiveness?

One Bell Telephone commercial portrays a retired couple seated at their kitchen table. Loneliness looms around them. Their family is gone. Subtle indications of emptiness and separation are apparent between parents and children.

The wife breaks the silence of the mundane, breakfast routine and says, "Joey called last night!"

It has been quite some time since they have heard from their son. How do we know? The father's startled response tells us.

"Was something wrong?" the father nervously inquires. "Is he sick? Are the children all right? Was there an emergency?"

These questions indicate that they never hear from the family unless there is trouble. Sound familiar to you? Have you ever said, "They only call when they want something"?

Had they not heard from their son because of an estranged relationship? Perhaps they are just out of touch with those they love.

Rather than growing together through the years, we often grow apart.

Do we really know each other, those closest to us—our parents, children, spouses, friends, brothers, sisters, family?

Many of us grow older never having known our own parents. Do you know what your parents' childhood was like? What were their favorite toys? What dreams filled their minds? What failures discouraged them? What were their fears, their aspirations? Who were they? Who were their childhood buddies and companions? What made life a fantasy for them? How did life's harsh realities alter their dreams? Do those closest to you know you? Has the essence of the significant other been discovered?

I have stood in funeral homes after performing services and heard wives, husbands, children, after hearing friends eulogizing the deceased say, "I never knew that side of my father/mother!"

Busy schedules, life's routines, often sidetrack us from deep interpersonal relationships.

The commercial ends by focusing in upon the mother's face, whose eyes have welled up with tears. Reaching for her husband's hand she says, "Joey called just to say, 'I love you, Mom!'"

Just to say I love you.

And husband and wife, at this breakfast table, acknowledge their deepest need to be loved, to hear it. And tenderly, they look into each other's eyes with the embraceable look of love.

I love you!

Just what each of us needs to say to someone every day.

What someone needs to say to us.

Taking the time to share love, that embraceable look, that word of encouragement, and to offer the gift of hope.

This is what Jesus does for you and me. He says, "I have come that you might have life. I have come just to tell you that I love you." His looking on us attests to this. It is a look of love.

Radio personality Paul Harvey caught my attention in the car one morning with the question, "When is the best time to tell your wife you love her?" Having gone through a divorce, I was curious and ready for his answer.

"Stay tuned for the answer following a commercial break."

I was impatient and curious in the morning traffic until Mr. Harvey's voice resumed with the question:

"When is the best time to tell your wife you love her?"

A slight pause followed to arouse the interest of the radio audience. *Come on,* I yelled to myself. *Out with the answer.*

The reply stunned me!

"Before somebody else does!"

I began to shake, feeling the empty pit in my stomach. Paul Harvey's interesting thought for the day evoked within me feelings most recently worked upon on my renewal journey. I had neglected to tell my wife I loved her, inattentive to her need for that embraceable look of love.

Somebody else told her that he loved her. And she married him, not too long after our divorce.

Charles Schulz, the creator of the Peanuts comic strip, presents Lucy in a tender moment with Charlie Brown. Lucy is plucking the petals of a daisy saying, as she glances affectionately at Charlie Brown seated comfortably under the shade of a tree,

> "He loves me, he loves me not;
> He loves me, he loves me not;
> He loves me, he loves me not;
> He loves me, he loves me not;
> *He loves me!!!!*
>
> Charlie Brown, you love me!"

Charlie Brown responds, "Gosh Lucy, I could have told you that!"

Remorsefully, Lucy replies, "Well, why didn't you Charlie Brown? Why didn't you?"

Why cannot we more easily and responsibly be attentive in expressing our feelings to others and to God? Human nature is so careless and remiss in sharing the love of the heart. If we habitually fail in expressing our love, in sharing the embraceable look of love, we miss the opportunity to fill another's life, and ours as well, with the wholeness that expressed love provides.

In "Things You Didn't Do," a young girl's poem in *Living, Loving and Learning,* author Leo Buscaglia shares the importance of the need to "embrace life now, and embrace one another" with the embraceable look of love before our thoughtlessness creates missed opportunities. The girl recounts many forgiven mistakes in her relationship with a young man, and then says,

> Remember the day I borrowed your brand new car and I
>   dented it?
> I thought you'd kill me, but you didn't.
> And remember the time I dragged you to the beach, and you
>   said it would rain, and it did?
> I thought you'd say. "I told you so," But you didn't.
> Do you remember the time I flirted with all the guys to
>   make you jealous, and you were?
> I thought you'd leave me, but you didn't.
> Do you remember the time I spilled strawberry pie all over
>   your car rug?
> I thought you'd hit me, but you didn't.
> And remember the time I forgot to tell you the dance was
>   formal and you showed up in jeans?
> I thought you'd drop me, but you didn't.
> Yes, there were lots of things you didn't do.
> But you put up with me, and you loved me, and you
>   protected me.
> There were lots of things I wanted to make up to you when
>   you returned from Viet Nam.
> BUT YOU DIDN'T.[3]

All of us need to be told we are loved. Tell people now of your love for them. If you have delayed and denied that gift of love for someone and as a result denied filling your own life with love, go to that parent, that child, brother, sister, friend, person at work, and tell your appreciation, your love, your care. Do not delay. Delays often bring regrets because delays can create missed opportunities.

I grew up not hearing the words I love you from my dad very often. Perhaps this was the root of my own inability to express my love in words.

Through our family's crises has come the blessing of hearts unfolding with new hues of love. While my dad found it difficult in the past to say, "I love you," within the past year and a half, he has done more out of love and expressed his love, making up for the years of not saying these words.

The following letter from my mom and dad is one I shall treasure all of my life. It was written out of our mutual journey through life's wilderness and uncertainties. It is the essence of what exists between people who love one another, express that love, and affirm that love.

Dear Ron,

Your message last night was soul searchingly meaningful, and filled one with much to think about in so many ways. We were truly proud and humbled to receive such a blessing from our very own Dear Son. There are never words to amply express how we feel about your amazing and obvious growth experience which comes through as it seems, from the very depths of your soul, and reaches everyone else who listens.

Sometimes our tears flow sadly and beautifully when we sit here and reflect at the wonder of you. Your wilderness shines through, more evidently in ways that only a right spirit could project, enabling you to reach the depth of one's soul.

God bless you for all that you were, all that you are, and for all that you will become.

Love, Mom and Dad

And looking upon them I will always love them. This letter was their way of embracing me with their look of love. And they have allowed me to look at myself in a new way. Loved and accepted just for who I am and what they believe I can become.

It is the same with Christ's love.

How can you begin to know that you are loved by God? Embraced by Him? Begin to perceive how He sees you. He will always look upon you with love, even if your eyes fall away from Him.

In *Lost Honor,* John Dean takes us through the maelstrom of public events and personal reckonings that followed his imprisonment for his involvement in the political scandal of Watergate. He was faced with the question of what he wanted to do with the rest of his life:

Constantly, since Watergate, I have been examining my life, but I now realize that my reassessment efforts have been misdirected. I have been making a "damage study," not an evaluation of who I am and what I am going to do. I have been asking questions like "Will people hold my past against me?" My view has been backward, not forward. And I have been dwelling on the trivial, or insignificant, too much. Time is running out and I must come to terms with my life. The days for fantasizing great achievements are gone. Ambitions and goals must be realistic if I want to avoid great disappointments at the end. What is important, John?[4]

Let us be realistic about our lives. If we want fulfillment, we must turn to God, who is the provider of all that is good and fulfilling.

John Dean said he made a major mistake in spending so much time doing a "damage study." Do you wallow in past mistakes, regrets, guilt? It is good to reexamine our lives, to discover ways we can realign ourselves with God's dreams for us. We can learn from our past. But we must be careful not to direct our energies there. If we do, our reassessment efforts will be misdirected. Our damage studies can keep us emotionally trapped in the past.

God forgives you of your past. He looks at you through an embraceable look of love. And in knowing that, you can look at yourself in a new way. People might hold your past against you. That is human nature. And it is our human nature to hold ourselves prisoner of our own pasts. The dark spots shadow us still.

What is needed in your life is to make the decision not to do a damage study but to move the shadows of our lives into the right perspective. For Christ and His embraceable look of love are bigger than any one of your problems. When He is magnified in your life, sin is not only minimized. It is forgiven. You are cleansed. You are restored to the loving embrace of God.

Our view of life must be forward. The apostle Paul put it another way: "Forgetting those things which are behind and reaching forward to those things which are ahead, I press toward the goal. . . ."[5]

God wants a new, fulfilling life for you!

John Dean's last question applies to all of us. "What is important?"

It was Reichel who said, "Not unless we fill our existence with an aim do we make it life." What matters most in life for you? Ambitions, wealth, riches, materialism? Fantasies which create worlds of illusions?

What are we aiming for in life? Personal satisfaction? Self-fulfillment? The concern for self-fulfillment through humanistic psychotherapy has produced what Peter Marin calls the "deified, isolated, self-centered self . . . lonely, vulnerable individuals encapsulated with false values."

Rollo May, the psychologist, says, "moving up the steps of self-actualization means moving from one level of internal development to a higher level within the self, rather than reaching beyond the self or outside the self. If we fail to do this we will suffer guilt because we have not developed our true potentials."

What do we want out of life?

The embraceable look of love from God will enable us to catch that vision of Himself and of our own lives so that what is actualized within us is the love He lives out through us. This is the only fulfilling sustaining quality of life. It is the essence of everything else.

To start afresh means to shift our vision to the healing presence and power of Christ who allows us to regain, or to gain for the first time, a new vision for life. We must ask ourselves the same question John Dean asked of himself: "What is important?"

Jesus asked it in a slightly different way when He met a blind man. "What do you want?" He asked the blind man. And we must respond as he did. "I want to see, to take a new look at myself, a look that will lead to a new life." A look that sees the embraceable look of God's love.

All of us carry the baggage of the past along with us. Each of us has the need to *release the valise*.

We need to release our grip on the damaging baggage of our past, which weighs heavily upon us, to release all that makes life lethargic.

Riding a bicycle for a while reminds us of how we can assume the posture of the position we take. Gliding along with hands gripped tightly to the handle bars, we discover that after an excursion of many miles that when we release our hands from the clutch of the handlebars our muscles have formed themselves to the curvature of the bar. We must pry open our fingers from the shape they have assumed from grasping the bars.

If you go through life holding on to a past that is filled with sin, problems, fears, and anxieties, your very personality will assume the character of those things you maintain in your grasp.

In releasing our past, in releasing the valise, the baggage that makes us spiritually apathetic, what must we grasp? We must grasp the embraceable look of God's love for us, and grasp His hand that will form us in His image and likeness.

My good friend, Chuck Colson, inspired me to see how one can learn to take a new look at himself when he sees himself through God's loving eyes. In *Born Again,* Chuck attests to this new life:

> As I was sitting in my car, the tears were flowing uncontrollably. . . . My sobbing was the only sound other than the chirping of crickets that penetrated the still of the night. With my face cupped in my hands, my head leaning forward against the wheel, I forgot about pretenses, about fears of being weak. And as I did, I began to experience a wonderful feeling of being released. Then came the strange sensation that water was not only running down my cheeks, but surging through my whole body as well, cleansing and cooling as it went. They weren't tears of sadness and remorse, nor of joy, but tears of relief. And then I prayed my first real prayer. "God, I don't know how to find you, but I'm going to try. Take me, take me." For the first time in my life I was not alone at all, at all.[6]

Chuck Colson was born again. Today he is lifting the lives of prisoners, through the ministry of Prison Fellowship, so that those captive behind bars and those family members held captive by the stigma of prison can grow to know the embraceable look of love.

And so, how does God view us? What does His looking upon us and loving us mean? Such a look tells us that He sees a deeper quality of goodness and love within all of us that we often do not perceive in ourselves or in others.

The immortal characters in the classic movie *The Wizard of Oz* bring us to a high moment of discovering this truth, when goodness and loveliness underlie what appears to be bad.

Dorothy, the Scarecrow, the Tin Man, and the Cowardly Lion finally return to the castle at Oz after having liquidated the wicked witch. They bring with them the accomplished task required by the fearsome Wizard, the burnt remains of the broom of the wicked witch.

Standing once again before the flames and smoke of the unapproachable holy place of the powerful Wizard, the intimidated characters present the broom and now beg of him to grant their requests, honoring his part of the bargain that would give the Scarecrow a brain, the Tin Man a heart, the Cowardly Lion courage, and Dorothy a way home.

The Wizard, hesitating in granting their wishes, arouses their indignation. During the ensuing interplay around the Wizard's power, authority, and intimidation, we suddenly notice Dorothy's pet dog Toto curious about the movement behind the suspicious curtain on the other side of the room.

After a few curious sniffs, Toto begins pulling the curtain open with his teeth, revealing a man shouting into a microphone and controlling all the gadgets that create the visual effects of the Wizard of Oz.

Dorothy says to the man behind the curtain, "Who are you?"

The embarrassed Wizard, played by Frank Morgan, shouts into the microphone, "I am the great . . . the great . . . the great and powerful, Wizard—of—Oz!"

"You are?" Dorothy cries out in defiance and rage.

The Wizard stands before them in complete humiliation.

"Why, you are nothing but a bad man," Dorothy proclaims.

And here the Wizard responds with the truth about the love of God found in the gospel, the truth that God is able to perceive greater qualities within people than they can see in themselves.

"Oh no, little girl. I am not a bad man. I am a good man. I'm just a terrible Wizard!"

I believe that there are no bad people. There are people who do bad things. Everyone in life is good! We might have done terrible things through wrong choices. Everyone is filled with the potential of God. No one is totally bad. Our eyes might even fall away from God. But His always fall upon us with an embraceable look of love.

What hope is there when we go around assuming that people are not good? That we are not good? The embraceable look of God's love reminds us that we are good people. And like Jesus, we need to look upon them and love them, upon ourselves, and love ourselves.

What must we look for in this embraceable look of God's love? The New Testament Book of Hebrews gives us our answer: "Let us lay aside every weight, and the sin which so easily ensnares *us,* and let us run with endurance the race that is set before us, looking unto Jesus, the author and finisher of *our* faith."[7] Today, lift up your eyes. Look to Jesus Christ. Tell Him you love Him! And walk with Him in His loving embrace.

CHAPTER 12

The Heart Exchange

"Our lives are made whole when hearts are exchanged at Calvary."

These words from Matthew Linn's *Healing Life's Hurts* affirm that we become whole individuals when we invite God into our hearts and lives. It is God's intention to change us, to give us life. At the cross that promise was made, the exchange provided. God took our sin and gave us His life in an exchange that will make us whole. If you let God embrace you, you will discover the joy expressed in Ezekiel 36:26:"I will give you a new heart and put a new spirit within you; I will take the heart of stone out of your flesh and give you a heart of flesh."

God will make you whole by exchanging His own heart with yours! In these days of miraculous medical technology, I am not referring to heart transplants to sustain the longevity of life. The heart exchange at Calvary literally creates new life and leads to an eternal relationship with God. "He or she who believeth in Me shall never die." "Never" the Scripture says! The heart exchange at Calvary is God's way of giving you everlasting life.

If this is the God you have made Lord of your life, He will give you everything that is His so that everything you are might be molded into spiritual wholeness.

In the chapter, "Death and Life," from James Michener's book, *The Source,* we are introduced to a time in biblical history when the Hebrews become loyal to false gods. These false gods, often carved in the form of clay figurines, are highlighted in this chapter in the form of the Canaanite goddess Astarte, the goddess of fertility. She was known to the Hebrews as Ashtoreth, to the Babylonians as Ishtar, to the Greeks as Aphrodite.

Michener repeatedly introduces this goddess as one who has tempted the Hebrews throughout all of Old Testament literature. He presents these gods in an historical age of uncertainty. Religious confusion and ambiguity has settled into a philosophy that includes many gods known as Baals. Monoliths are constructed to honor them, statues to which prayers are offered daily.

Astarte, the tempting goddess of fertility, was the one goddess that all of Makor revered. In this agricultural society she is significant, for without her, there would be no cycle of life.

Michener's main character is a young man named Urbaal, who was the head of the clan in Makor. Interestingly enough, his own name has within it the word for "god," Baal. We soon discover that he has made of himself, through his own pride and selfishness, a god. Urbaal adores the goddess Astarte. He feels powerless without her.

Among his many wives is one named Timna. She is loving, considerate, and understanding, to a point. As the chapter unfolds we discover her despair over the knowledge that she will be required to sacrifice her firstborn son to Astarte.

Urbaal tells her that "as long as Makor has existed we have delivered to the gods our firstborn sons. And you shall too."

In this dilemma, James Michener unravels the anguish over the conflict between life and death.

> On the platform in the temple stood a stone god of unusual construction. It has two extended arms raised so that from the stone fingertips to the body they formed a wide inclined plane. Whoever was placed upon the arms was free to roll swiftly downward and plunge into the fire. With trembling turns, as if he were a little ball, her infant son dropped into the flames.[1]

Grief for her son becomes immersed in the grief she now feels as she watches her husband's enchantment over a temple prostitute who is awarded to him for his abundant harvests.

All the while Timna struggles with her own conscience and values. As she watches her husband, she reviews the principles by which she has lived. From her previous experiences, outside Makor before she met her husband, she was able to entertain the concept that beyond this village was another world, a better life, a different God.

Timna, grieving for her son and now watching the performance of her husband with the temple prostitute says, "What folly!" She walks home, seeing life in its painful clarity. She goes into his "god-room," looks with abhorrence at the four Astartes and smashed them along with their phallic companions. It is here that she utters these words, highlighting the difference a heart exchange can make in one's life: "Had he a different God, he would have been a different man."[2]

When we have God in our lives we become different people. All of us desire to be whole, complete, different, new! Everyone wants to grow. Our example for this growth is Jesus Christ. Remember His words: "Follow me and I will make you!"

Recently I read the story of John D. Rockefeller in the *Encyclopedia of Illustrations*. John D. Rockefeller, Sr., was a strong and husky boy. He determined early to earn money, and he drove himself to the limit. At age thirty-three, he earned his first million dollars. At age forty-three, he controlled the biggest company in the world. At age fifty-three, he was the richest man on earth and the world's only billionaire.

Then he developed a disease called alopecia, the hair of his head dropped off, and his eyelashes and eyebrows disappeared. He virtually seemed to wither away. His weekly income was one million dollars, but he digested only milk and crackers. He was so hated in Pennsylvania that he had to have bodyguards day and night. He could not sleep, stopped smiling altogether, and enjoyed nothing in life.

The doctors predicted he would not live over one year. The newspaper had gleefully written his obituary in advance— for convenience in sudden use. Those sleepless nights set him thinking. He realized with a new light that he "could not take one dime into the next world." Money was not everything.

The next morning found him a new man. He began to help churches with his amassed wealth; the poor and needy were not overlooked. He established the Rockefeller Foundation which funded medical research leading to the discovery of penicillin and other wonder drugs. John D. began to sleep well, eat, and enjoy life.

The doctors had predicted he would not live over age fifty-four. He lived to see ninety-eight.

John D. Rockefeller literally became a new man because he found a new God. He had a heart exchange. He was made whole. He lived a full life, not because he was ninety-eight but because God made him whole.

It is God's desire to exchange hearts with us so that we might build the character of our lives in His image. For many people it is difficult to comprehend God's willingness to love them to the point of completely changing them.

John Calvin conveys to us God's intention despite our weaknesses, our sin: "that we are fallen creatures and like fallen creatures we are cracked cathedrals. The windows may be shattered, the steeple may be leaning, the cathedral may be no more than a desolate ruin; but it is still a cathedral." Yes, we are cracked cathedrals. Jesus also said our bodies are His temple and that He would place within our hearts His love. We are still God's children, created in His likeness and image. There is not only potential goodness within us. There is inherent goodness within us. He loves us enough to rebuild us. Our lives can be reconstructed when our lives are reconciled and our hearts exchanged for God's at Calvary.

Many times I am asked about my feelings towards my former spouse. Am I held prisoner to animosity or anger? What grudges and grievances still play back in my recorded memory? Have I been able to forgive in a creative process? Has God been able to heal the wounds?

I have had to learn to view and answer these questions from a rather unique and difficult position. While the questions are directed at me in such a way that it would be easy and comfortable to make myself the innocent and injured party, they also remind me that my former wife and I still have a common union.

Both of us were dealing with the same anger, pain, wounds, and hurts caused by the other. And both of us were being loved, sustained, strengthened and renewed by the same gracious, loving, and guiding God, whose concern it was that we be whole and healed individuals.

The God who was walking with me through my wilderness was the same Creator who designed a wonderful, full, and happy life for my former wife. And therefore I could not stand in judgment of her, nor she of me. In our faith journey both of us were standing before a loving God, who I am sure was compassionately dealing with us, even though disappointed with our inability to reconcile our relationship and allow Him to make the exchange within our hearts that would have led to healing. God not only heals broken hearts. He can heal broken relationships when two persons share a joint commitment to each other and a full commitment to Him.

Hatred was not an issue in our marriage. Complacency about developing trust and commitment was. But as a couple we must have inflicted enough pain upon each other that our relationship had to be severed. That pain came from a lack of trust within the relationship or a total complacency in meeting each other's needs. I made major contributions to the mistrust in this relationship.

Fortunately, divorce does not mean you are disconnected from life. In gaining new perspectives about yourself and a clearer understanding of God's sustaining love, your life can be made whole if you give your heart to God.

I recall an image and a moment which speaks to me now of painful growth in order for new life to emerge.

God's love was revealed to me in a labor room and a delivery room when my wife was giving birth to our second daughter, Sarah. During my wife's breathing exercises, intended to alleviate her pain, Christ's forgiving love was revealed to me. Pain twisted my wife's face into a look I had seen not only once before, but on many different occasions. As I soothed her discomfort with massages to her back, that look of pain continued to speak to me. How peculiar it must sound to you that I saw Christ in the labor room, etched over my wife's pain-twisted face.

Here was a woman giving birth to our second gift of

God's creation. And all the time a birthing process was happening with me also.

It was her look.

It was her pain.

A look of pain that I had inflicted many times, when in stubborn pride I used angry words as a power play to gain the upper hand. The hurting comments used to knock her down a few pegs or pull the carpet of support or love from beneath her. The pain I saw in her face as she gave birth was pain I often inflicted upon her myself when my love was absent or unexpressed.

Labor pain is not the hardest pain we must bear. The pain we inflict upon each other often is.

The same pain I saw on my wife's face I have seen on my Lord's face each time I do something that grieves Him, each time I sin and fall short of His love, each time I try to get the upper hand by proclaiming my will over His will. Letting my pride make of me, god, rather than my life making of Him, Lord.

Yet etched in His face, I saw, as I saw in my wife's face, the lifting power of His love that comes to give you and me new life, new birth, new hope, forgiveness. In that heart exchange at Calvary, in the pain of our Lord's face, comes our new birth that makes our life whole. It is our sin He bore. And His love was born in us.

My wife and I mutually caused each other pain. When she petitioned for divorce, my complacency about commitment and trust cost me a great depth of emotional trauma—anger, resentment, and hatred. These are destructive attitudes in anyone's emotional and spiritual development. In fact the emotional dynamics of grief in the divorce process will allow hatred to run wild with illusions of the other person's death. It would be easier if something tragic would happen rather than have to deal with the pain of divorce and "having to see her face again."

How could I remain emotionally secure as a man, a man who now resented and hated the thought of the very image of a woman who had been my wife for fifteen years and was still now the mother of my two daughters? I was literally nauseated at the thought of her name. Twisted knots of anger caused me great inner stress and vacillating levels of anxiety throughout each day.

What integrity would there be to my ministry and to my own faith with cruel hate pervading and overriding all that I preached from God's word and believed within my own life? Yet in trying to obliterate these destructive, negative, emotionally incapacitating feelings, I could not remove myself from the rut of my despair. No matter how many times I told myself that I had forgiven her and asked God for my own forgiveness, I still contained the grudges within and felt unworthy about myself before the all-forgiving one God to whom I was praying daily. There was a deepseated resistance to relinquishing my hatred.

How then, was I to move on to the new levels of life God was planning for me? I was the one who needed a heart exchange. My life was not whole. The realization that wholeness would come when I admitted that I could not forgive, but that God's forgiveness could work within me brought my life in direct confrontation with the cross. My faith was at its testing point! Would I open my heart to God's healing, releasing my festering hatred?

I needed to be set free! Even the knowledge of Scripture caused warfare within my mind. I knew well the words from Colossians 1:11–14: May you be "strengthened with all might, according to His glorious power. . . . He has delivered us from the power of darkness and translated *us* into the kingdom of the Son of His love, in whom we have redemption. . . ." But they were not truth for me. Spiritual impotency ruled my spirit. My hatred maintained only one strong position in my life, the position of a helpless, enfeebled faith. If God's glorious power was to enter my heart, I needed to exchange that enfeebled faith with the strength that comes from His love that would set me free.

But how?

I was weak in my faith! God knew it. I needed to tell Him.

The apostle Paul says, "I will all the more gladly boast of my weakness, that the power of Christ may rest upon me." I admitted my cancerous hatred. Christ's presence was with me. Yet no immediate answer was provided. The struggle lasted for weeks. Thinking of Jacob's wrestling till the break of day made me wonder when the dawn would rise in my life.

Then one day, when my mind was not even thinking

about this inner struggle, I picked up Corrie Ten Boom's book, *The Hiding Place*. Her story introduced me, in a clear way, to the heart exchange that would give her the power of forgiveness and direct me to discover that truth for myself. Years after her concentration camp experiences during the World War, in which her sister Betsie and her father were executed, she was confronted with the vivid memory of that horrific moment. She was speaking at a church service on the topic of forgiveness.

> It was at a church service in Munich that I saw him, the former S.S. man who had stood guard at the shower room door in the processing center at Ravensbruck. He was the first of our actual jailers that I had seen since that time. And suddenly it was all there—the roomful of mocking men, the heaps of clothing. Betsie's pain-blanched face.
>
> He came up to me as the church was emptying, beaming and bowing. "How grateful I am for your message, Fraulein," he said. "To think that, as you say, He has washed my sins away!"
>
> His hand was thrust out to shake mine. And I, who had preached so often to the people in Bloemendaal the need to forgive, kept my hand at my side. Even as the angry, vengeful thoughts boiled through me, I saw the sin of them. Jesus Christ had died for this man; was I going to ask more? Lord Jesus, I prayed, forgive me and help me to forgive him.
>
> I tried to smile, I struggled to raise my hand. I could not. I felt nothing, not the slightest spark of warmth or charity. And so again, I breathed a silent prayer. "Jesus, I cannot forgive him. Give me your forgiveness."
>
> As I took his hand the most incredible thing happened. From my shoulder along my arm and through my hand a current seemed to pass from me to him, while into my heart sprang a love for this stranger that almost overwhelmed me.
>
> And so I discovered that it is not on our forgiveness anymore than on our goodness that the world's healing hinges, but on His. When He tells us to love our enemies, He gives, along with the command, the love itself.[3]

There was my answer. God gives, along with the command to love and forgive, the love and forgiveness itself. I could not forgive my wife until a heart exchange occurred at Calvary. I gave to God my heart of anger, hatred, and resentment. He gave me His heart full of love, compassion, and forgiveness.

Shortly thereafter I was celebrating Communion with my congregation at the morning worship service. It was the first time in nearly two years that I mentally uttered the words and silently repeated them on my lips, "Lord, create within me a clean heart." Repeating her full, newly married name, I asked that God would forgive my former spouse and prayed earnestly that God would continue His healing forgiveness within me.

The heart exchange at that moment set me free of my hatred. New life and wholeness is a pledged promise from God. John 5:24 assures us that the person "who hears My word and believes in Him who sent Me has everlasting life."

If you leave your heart open for the life-exchanging experience at Calvary, trusting God to give you His love, you will have an abundant life in the grace and joy of the Spirit.

Perhaps you are reluctant to give your heart fully to God. Even unwilling!

But even an unwilling heart can be changed!

The founder of the United Methodist Church, John Wesley, reveals the loving nature of God that leads you to a heart-warming experience. His journal articulates God's grace which has the ability to change your life, even if at first you appear to be unwilling to allow Him to completely and fully enter your heart. In John Wesley's unwillingness we discover God's willingness to renew us. We read in his journal:

> In the evening, I went very unwillingly to a society small group meeting in Aldersgate-street where one was reading Luther's preface to the Epistle to the Romans. About a quarter before nine, while he was describing the change which God works in the heart through faith in Christ, I felt my heart strangely warmed. I felt I did trust in Christ, Christ alone, for my salvation. And an assurance was given to me that he had taken away my sins.[4]

John Wesley had been disenchanted with his spiritual life. In fact he was floundering in his faith. Notice! He went *unwillingly* to Aldersgate-street. Perhaps he did not want to go at all. Yet, a still, small voice inspired him to go. In his unwillingness we discover the power of God to warm the heart with faith through the hearts that are exchanged at Calvary. God Himself leads those who have gone astray to repentance. As Psalm 23:3 says, "He leads me in the paths of righteousness." God can lead you into that moment of wholeness, when through His will and through the power of the Holy Spirit, His love is exchanged with your heart. God works within unwilling lives.

If you are slightly unwilling to fully give your life to Jesus Christ, bring that unwilling attitude to the Cross and discover the willingness of God to make your life whole. Your life will be strong as you exchange your heart with God's. And as you continue to look to Him for guidance and wisdom, you will be a winner!

Simply turn your life to Jesus Christ. He is waiting to give you His heart.

What a tremendous musical event it was to hear the Berlin Symphony Orchestra in Carnegie Hall perform a Brahms symphony under the direction of Herbert von Karijan.

During one of the movements the serenity of the setting was penetrated by the reverberating snap of a string on the first chair's violin. My third row seat, center orchestra provided me with a view of an ensuing situation that would become for me a symbol of God's ability to be a constant help in trouble, of God's ability to exchange with us the love that will mend broken hearts.

With one string broken, the moment intensified the frustration and anxiety as a second string snapped back across the musician's shoulder.Calmly, but with an emphatic disappointment, the violinist placed his incapacitated instrument at the side of his chair. As he searched his pants pockets, then his shirt pocket and inside jacket pockets, I became keenly aware of the musician's embarrassment.

He had no package of spare strings. Frustration was etched on his face. He could do nothing but sit idly by while von Karajan continued to conduct.

Then the symbol of redemption, of God's intervening love, was demonstrated before my very eyes.

From the second row of violins a hand tapped the shoulder of the disabled musician. They whispered to each other and then exchanged violins.

The first-chair violinist reentered the next measure in the score of music with the borrowed violin while the second musician reached into his tuxedo jacket and took out a plastic bag of strings.

A second tap on the shoulder indicated the repairs had been made. Both musicians exchanged violins and blended into harmony with the rest of the orchestra.

Our lives are made whole when hearts are exchanged at Calvary. When our lives are broken, shattered, seemingly beyond repair, we feel the loving tap of Christ, placing His finger of hope upon our lives.

When the last thread of hope snaps, He intervenes with a grace that is sufficient for renewal. As our lives are turned over to His care and remaking, we are handed back a healed life with power to continue to grow in His love. Our power for living comes from feeling the tap of God's loving hand upon our lives, from the embrace of His love.

We can turn over to Him what we have the inability to handle on our own. Like Corrie Ten Boom, we can hand Him our inability to forgive and find, along with His command to love, the love itself.

And what will you receive when He gives you your life? "A new heart He will give you and a new spirit He will put within you."

Is there someone in your life you cannot forgive, someone who has hurt you? Do you carry the grudge in your heart? Stand at the cross, the place where the heart exchange becomes effective. There God's redeeming work is done.

He will take you into His loving embrace. He will forgive you and enable you to forgive others. For He will fill your life with the love you need. He wants to give you His heart!

Is anything preventing your doing this? Are you stubbornly resistant to Him? What is deterring you from expressing your feelings to Him, or exchanging your heart with His?

Let the Scripture inspire you:

> Today, if you will hear His voice,
> Do not harden your hearts as in the rebellion.[5]

Open your heart! Now. Let His loving embrace come in.

CHAPTER 13

God, Can We Talk?

Comedienne Joan Rivers has a trademark one-liner in her comic monologue, a statement that draws thunderous applause: "Can we talk?"

In three words Ms. Rivers moves from comic monologue to a brief glimpse of serious dialogue with her audience.

Prayer is our ability to *get serious* with life, with ourselves, and with God. Not briefly. Unceasingly. We need to approach God simply by saying, "God, can we talk?" and move into life's most creative dialogue and faith's most endearing relationship.

"Can we talk?" will lead us in prayer to life's most intimate embrace—complete oneness with God! In this unity with God we find peace.

Talking with God through prayer helps us to keep our minds open to Him. Prayer focuses us on God and opens our lives to what He has designed for us. If we would have peace and quiet for our troubled souls, we must be disciplined in prayer. Like the apostle Paul, we must pray unceasingly until prayer molds our peace.

Prayer will not always compress us into calmness nor satisfy every desire. But it will open us to God's healing touches.

And it will provide a way for God's will to be done in and through our lives. It will sustain us as we have to wait patiently for many answers. Through prayer, we will find our minds always clearing and our souls discovering quietness and peace.

La Bruyere says that "most people spend much of their lives making the rest of their lives miserable." We can create more problems for ourselves and carry around with us many unnecessary burdens that weigh us down in our pilgrimage through this marathon called life.

Prayer gives wings to our lives. Through it we are lifted closer to God. It is the key that opens the door to God's embrace.

PRAYER PROVIDES A REAL ENCOUNTER AND NURTURES A LOVING EMBRACE WITH GOD.

We encounter God in many ways. He is most real in our prayer life. We hear Him more clearly when we are alone with Him in prayer. In this intense encounter we are made aware of His constant care.

We are not the only ones who ask of Him, "Can we talk?" It is God's desire to be open and available to us. From the Creator we hear the same question. His desire is to be close. Be still and know Him as God. You will hear Him say: *"Can We Talk?"* God wants to be intimate with us. He yearns to embrace us with His love.

The encounter with God in prayer gives us strength for living. Without prayer we are not in touch nor in tune with His will. Engaging our lives in prayerful dialogue with God will provide us with limitless power for creative living. Rollo May, in *The Courage to Create,* says,

> The first thing we notice in a creative art is that it is an encounter. Artists encounter the landscape they propose to paint. They look at it, observe it from this angle and that. They are as we say, absorbed in it. Or, in the case of abstract painters, the encounter may be with an idea, an inner vision; a healthy child's play also has the essential features of encounter, and we know it is one of the important prototypes of adult creativity. The essential point is the degree of absorption, the degree of intensity; there must be a specific quality of engagement.[1]

Without prayer, life is spiritually shallow. With prayer, God can profoundly change us and help us grow. Prayer is an intense encounter that absorbs us in the presence of God, a complete encounter with him. Without it there can never be abundant life.

PRAYER BUILDS A DEEP FAITH FOUNDATION

Standing at the construction site of the new Marriott Hotel complex in Times Square, I observed the analogy between the rising of a great skyscraper and the stature of faith created by prayer. At an excavation site you can determine the height of the skyscraper by the depth of the foundation being created. The deeper the foundation, the higher the building.

As steel pilings are driven into the ground to lay a foundation, the driving force of prayer within our lives is the foundation upon which we build our faith. The deeper your prayer life, the stronger your faith and relationship to God. You become better equipped to face life.

The Empire State Building is 102 stories high, with a foundation five floors below street level. The famous Twin Towers, known as the World Trade Center, is 107 stories high with a foundation eight floors below street level. The deeper your prayer life, the taller you will stand.

Each time you talk with God, the stronger you become. Prayer will embrace you with power.

A WEAK PRAYER LIFE PRODUCES A WEAK LIFE

The Japanese have created a beautiful horticultural phenomenon in dwarfed bonzai trees. Their beauty was caused by a mutation, a stunting of their growth in order to form the appeal for which they are famous and expensive.

The technique used for designing these plants consists of removing the soil from the intricate network of rootlets. The taproot, once segregated, is wrapped with a wire, tying off the flow of rich nourishment from the soil to the plant.

Why constrict the taproot?

It is the taproot which penetrates the deepest in the soil.

Through it the greatest amount of nourishment is provided for plant growth.

Once the root is tied, the plant begins surviving from the nutrients drawn in through the surface roots. These rootlets never reach down beyond their own shallowness. Thus is created a beautiful plant, deceptive to the eye. While they appear to be beautiful creations, some of them existing for hundreds of years through surface roots, their growth has actually been stunted.

Many people go through life giving the appearance that all is well, blissful, and happy. Yet many are living only from surface roots.

Without prayer in our lives we cut ourselves off from reaching deeply within the wonderful resources of God's love which He provides for our growth in faith. If we live on surface roots, relying on faith occasionally or superfically, we will never grow into the stature and wisdom of faith.

Developing a deeply committed prayer life, rooted in the grace and love of God, we will always be strong:

> He shall be like a tree
> Planted by the rivers of water, That brings forth its fruit
>   in its season,
> Whose leaf also shall not wither;
> [you won't be stunted]
> And whatever he does shall prosper.[2]

If you want power for living, move beyond a surface relationship with God and build a deep foundation of faith in Him through prayer: "As you have therefore received Christ Jesus the Lord, so walk in Him, rooted and built up in Him and established in the faith."[3]

DON'T BE AFRAID TO PRAY—
JUST TALK WITH GOD

Many people fear prayer because they assume prayer must be laced with godly talk. I like the person who allows prayer to be simple, conversational, clearly articulated, honest, open, relevant, and personal.

Our fear in praying is due to the fact that we expose the

depth of our private world. Our soul is personal territory. We are afraid to be discovered.

Will we be accepted? Loved? Forgiven? Not so much by God, but by others who might perceive us with a critical eye? It is difficult enough to have God uncover and unravel the depths of our hearts. No one else needs to gain a glimpse of our inner selves.

Those who are reluctant to pray publicly feel that a theological degree which results in ecclesiastical prayers is needed. As a result the minister is looked to as the one providing words for grace and comfort. He's trained. He should be eloquent. And after all it's his job!

Fear of praying crippled me significantly at an early age. At thirteen, after attending a youth group for several weeks, I was aware of the customary ritual of praying at the end of each meeting. The prayer was offered by one of the youths who was selected by the president of the youth group.

In fearful anticipation of being called upon to pray, I pulled the president of the group to the side one evening and told him not to call upon me—*ever!* I did not know how to pray. I was afraid to pray.

The evening's activities went well until we joined our hands for the closing prayer circle. A frozen wave of fear traveled quickly through my body when I heard, "Will Ron Cadmus please lead us in the closing prayer?" Tears began welling up in my eyes. Words were caught in my throat. My mind went blank. How could he have betrayed me? My entrapment in the hands of those next to me prevented a quick flight from the room.

Trembling, and after a pause equivalent to eternity, my lips began to separate with utterances unintelligible.

> Thank you God—
> for the
> sun,
> the moon,
> the flowers,
> the rain that makes the flowers grow
> the fields,
> the birds,
> for my mom and dad,
> for my pet dog, Rusty!

The group erupted into laughter, a painful introduction to humiliation. It was the last time I actively participated with the group.

Ten years later, when I was behind a desk in my seminary dorm, doing exegetical work on the Psalms, God revealed to me the simple essence of prayer, in words uttered by another young man of faith:

> He causes the grass to grow for cattle,
> and vegetation for the service of man,
> That he may bring forth food from the earth . . .
> And bread *which* strengthens man's heart.
> The trees of the LORD are full *of sap* . . .
> Where the birds make their nests. . . .
> The earth is full of Your possessions—
> This great and wide sea,
> In which *are* innumerable teeming things.[4]

It was a moment of resolve for me, dissolving my fear of praying in the simple truth of prayer, praise, and thanksgiving. Here was the psalmist praying about things I had prayed about at thirteen— animals, sun, moon, rain, water, grass, birds!

Prayer in its sublime simplicity! It is important just to say to God "Can we talk?" and just talk—heart to heart!

LET PRAYER CENTER YOU ON GOD

Singer John Denver sings a popular country song entitled "Looking for Space." He expresses the need to look in the center of our lives to find the quality of life that encourages us through life's transitions.

> On the road of experience
> I'm trying to find my own way.
> Sometimes I wish that I could fly away. . . .
> Then I look in the center
> Suddenly everything's clear.[5]

Prayer places us in touch with the center of our lives, and at the center of our lives we discover God. Christ is the center of your life. When you look in the center, suddenly everything is clear. You find yourself in the Son and Him within you.

Prayer claims Him as Lord of your life. Let prayer lead you to the center of your life. You will meet God there, waiting and ready to embrace you and lift you to soar with eagles.

PRAYER'S EMBRACE BRINGS YOU CLOSE TO GOD'S WORD

Just moments before the overture was completed and the curtain was raised for the first act of Yul Brynner's *The King and I,* the usher escorted a couple to the vacant seats next to me in the third row, center orchestra.

They were blind. My curiosity was aroused. Why would blind people spend forty-five dollars on front row orchestra seats? Seemed a waste of money.

I peripherally observed their excitement throughout the musical. They were sensitive to every word. Suddenly I began realizing a truth that my own blindness had prevented me from seeing.

This couple responded to each subtle line of humor before others around them heard the dialogue.

A keen sense of hearing enabled them to be moved at the very depth of tenderness in the passion expressed between the King of Siam and Anna. This couple was seeing and feeling many things that most of us were missing or became aware of through a delayed response.

They displayed a parallel between prayer and the position we take in our relationship to God. They didn't sit where they could see best. Whether they were in front row center orchestra seats or last row "up with the angels" made no difference. Darkness created the same distance. Instead, they sat where they could best hear every word from the actors on stage.

In prayer, we come directly to the feet of God. His closeness provides us with His loving embrace. Prayer places us center stage with God and God within the center of our lives. Position is everything. Closeness to Him determines how much we will hear His will for our lives.

There is no acoustical problem in hearing God's word. The communication problem often stems from the fact that we position ourselves away from God.

When we say "Can we talk?" to God, we make the move to bridge the gap. To move closer to Him. To be wrapped in His embrace. Without prayer in your life you cannot be close to God. Without Him you will have no power for living.

PRAYER CAN BE LETHAL

In the garden of Gethsemane, the night before Jesus was crucified, Jesus said to his disciples, "Pray, lest you fall into temptation." Prayer has a power over evil. It is lethal.

C. S. Lewis' *Screwtape Letters* introduces us to Screwtape, a devil who is training young Wormwood, his novice nephew. Screwtape is to provide the young, inexperienced destroyer of good with the techniques necessary to undermine the influence of faith in Christians.

Wormwood, however diligently he tries, continues to botch up his efforts. He cannot seem to defuse the power of these lovers of God.

A disgruntled Screwtape, in giving young Wormwood a few keys to certain success says, "The best thing, where it is possible, is to keep the patient from the serious intention of praying altogether. It is funny how mortals always picture us as putting things into their minds: in reality our best work is done by keeping things out."[5]

Screwtape affirms that prayer is lethal to evil's cause.

"At all costs, do not let these people pray to their God. For prayer is lethal to our cause."

Evil has no power over prayer.

Temptation will always attempt to break down the power of God within your life. A life without prayer is "open season" for the Screwtapes and Wormwoods that lurk over our shoulders and gently whisper in our ears.

The necessity for an energetic prayer life builds a faith that will not yield to temptation.

> Yield not to temptation for yielding is sin
> Each vict'ry will help you some other to win
> Fight courageously onward,
> Dark passions subdue
> Look ever to Jesus, He will carry you through.

To Him, that o'ercometh God giveth a crown
Thro' faith we shall conquer, though often cast down;
He who is our Saviour, our strength will renew,
Look ever to Jesus, He will carry you through.

Ask the Savior to help you, comfort,
strengthen and keep you.
He is willing to aid you,
He will carry you through.

Ask God in prayer to strengthen you. He will embrace you and carry you through life.

PERSIST IN PRAYER EVEN WHEN ANSWERS DON'T COME

Romans 12:9–12 says that we should be "not lagging in diligence, fervent in spirit, serving the Lord; rejoicing in hope, patient in tribulation, continuing steadfastly in prayer."

Adelle Jefferson never flagged in zeal. She was patient in tribulation and constant in prayer.

When I visited with her in a nursing home shortly before she died, Adelle reminisced with me about her mother who had been dead for many years.

As a young woman in her forties, Adelle took care of her aged mother, who was confined to a mental institution. Daily Adelle walked two and a half miles in faithful devotion to visit her mother.

Senility prevented the woman from recognizing her daughter. Nevertheless Adelle was devoted to these visits, knowing that she received much comfort from comforting her ailing mother and hoping that her mom could at least sense the presence of her love.

For seven years Adelle made this walk of faith and love.

For seven years her steadfast devotion and her faithful prayers were made with the hope for a sign of recognition.

It was a beautiful spring day. Freshly blossoms adorned the cherry trees lining the hospital roadway. Today's journey was to reveal God's continued unfolding love and hope for his faithful children.

Adelle walked across the lush green lawns of the hospital, seeing her mother in a wheel chair, cooled in the shade of surrounding trees.

She was frail and immobile, her gray hair blew loosely as dried wisps in the gentle breezes.

A draped shawl warmed her slumped shoulders and drooping head.

As Adelle approached her mother's frail, shaking body, the head lifted, with squinting, inquisitive eyes.

The tender touch of God's miracle was given this day to the longing heart of a faithful daughter. For upon her ears fell the words of love: "Here's my little girl."

The first words spoken in seven years. An eternity of persistent, faithful prayer through tribulation and heartache. Agonizing months of devotion. Finally an answer to prayer.

Life's victories come from being steadfast and immovable in faith.

Adelle told me the importance of the lesson learned through unceasing prayer.

"It was important to learn that even though there was a strong possibility that Mother would never recognize me, it was more important that the Lord find me faithful and trusting, steadfast and loyal to the power and discipline of prayer. In my prayer life, I found myself becoming closer to Him. At the end of my life, this still matters most.

"I discovered that He always knew who I was. He continually hears my prayers. My needs are known by Him. My life has been upheld through prayer, even if I never received the answers I desired. The lesson! To faithfully walk each day to meet Him in prayer. To see His outstretched arms and run into that loving embrace."

Three weeks after she told me this story, Adelle died. My spiritual eyes see her held in God's tender grasp, her head on His shoulder, His hand lovingly upon her head in love's greatest embrace. Prayer is the bond.

PRAYER: QUIET TIME'S EMBRACE

"Be still and know that I am God!"

We live hectic lives! Find time for God? We have just about enough freedom to spend quality time with our families or to provide ourselves with the necessary space for relaxation and enjoyment.

Better jobs, more money.

Longer hours, overtime income.

Families starve for affection. Children miss their parent's availability. Time speeds by quickly. The essence of life is missed. As we draw to the close of our lives, we wonder if they have been spent with the good intentions of making life productive and emotionally bountiful.

What do you do with your time? Do you race through life, or is each day interspersed with productive moments in addition to the mere routine of labor and the drudgery of survival?

"You Americans are all alike!" The accusation was thrust upon my friend Frank Fowler and myself as we hurriedly left an art museum in London, which we visited during our West Virginia Choir Tour of Europe.

We only had a half hour before we were set to leave for our next concert hall, so we quickly moved through the revolving doors of the museum's entrance and almost literally did a 360-degree turn, catching a glimpse of the art work, while we made our exit. We chuckled under a twinge of embarrassment when the guard at the door said, "You two must be Americans!"

"Why?" I asked.

"You Americans are all alike—always in a hurry! You never take the time to appreciate anything."

That happened in 1970. The memory is still imbedded in my mind today, reminding me that when my life becomes fast-paced, I often miss the beauty and the essence of the moment by rushing rapidly through it. Even my prayer life had evolved into a 360-degree, revolving-door relationship with God. In and out quickly to the throne of grace. Just enough time to catch a glimpse of Him, share a fleeting word with Him, then back to my own affairs, catching the next appointment. My schedule left little space for God.

In my hurry I was passing by stars. Missing the glimpses into the will and way of God. Taking little time to grasp either stars or Him.

I began learning about all those things I was missing when I came face to face with a star.

Placing your hand on a star! Looking through the door to the Kingdom of God! Have you ever imagined that you could reach for the stars and grasp them, or come so close to the Kingdom of God that you could peer through the door which leads to the eternal?

Often we do not pause long enough to know that it is possible not only to see stars but to grasp them.

A visit to the Church of the Nativity in Bethlehem provided me with the opportunity to touch a star. To gain a glimpse of abundance through the narrow gate that leads to a whole life. The very place where Jesus was born is marked by a star, a brilliant, twelve-pointed, silver star on the floor beneath the altar. It commemorates the spot where God became Emmanuel—God with us!

On bended knee, like those shepherds of long ago and the countless millions who have made the pilgrimage these two thousand years since, I gently placed my fingertips on the star, the place which birthed the miracle that would change the course of history and renew our personal lives. My touch was gentle yet purposeful, earnest in its intention to bring the Lord Jesus into my life in a way I never had before or experienced.

This was the place of swaddling clothes. It was a quiet, still moment in which I was swaddled in God's embrace. It was a moment to savor. It was the place where God came rushing to fill humanity's deepest need and longing.

After prayer, I rose to my feet and walked out of the manger stall, down a hallway, past a roped-off corridor, which led to a curious place. With no one in sight, I unlatched the rope which blocked entrance to an area marked by the ominous directive—"No trespassing."

I wanted to explore this curious hallway. Walking upon the rough flooring, apparently under excavation, the winding hallway led to an area with no exit. As I glanced down the dimly lit passageway, I saw an old, weathered, wooden door on the left wall. On tiptoe, I hesitated. I found myself in front of a small, barricaded doorway.

My eyes searched the texture of the door as my hands slid across the wood, until my hand touched the worn remains of a keyhole. Bending down to glance through, I was stunned to discover I was now on the opposite side of the manger stall, under-neath the church, an area yet to be opened to the public. In amazement, I looked through the keyhole to the place where Jesus had been born. The manger was dimly lit in reverence and adoration by candles, whose smell of beeswax flowed through the crevices of the wooden door.

I touched a star! The place where Jesus was born of Mary.

A glimpse through the keyhole gave me a peek into eter-nity. The door to faith is a narrow door, like the eye of a needle. It is a straight and narrow path, leading to the Savior, who was born for us and who gives us the grace to be "born again!"

The keyhole focused my vision to a narrow point, di-rectly upon the place where Jesus was born. Was this the original entrance to the manger? Was this the doorway through which the angels and shepherds came?

I am not really sure. But for me, it was the place where the door of my heart opened in all of its fullness to let Jesus Christ in. It was a moment that enriched my life. It was an expe-rience that required constant pondering. This was no 360-degree, revolving door moment. It was a time that would lead to eternity.

Prayer keeps our lives heavenward, toward stars! In touch with God. It opens the door to God's kingdom. It is the place where we need spend not just a lot of time, but all of our life.

Wouldn't it be great if it could be said of us, "You Chris-tians are all alike. You spend so much time in prayer!"

How many minutes a day do you spend praying? Does your prayer life change your time into life? Is your life fruitful because you spend time in prayer? If you prayed unceasingly, what a creative life you would have.

But life speeds by so quickly, and we spend so little time in prayer. Neglecting this aspect of our spiritual journey, we will not grow. Life will remain the same.

Lewis Carol in *Alice in Wonderland* provides us with a scene where the queen introduces Alice to a fact of modern life. Unfortunately, it is a present-day story about our lives.

Alice never could quite make out, in thinking it over afterwards, how it was that they began; all she remembers is that they were running hand in hand, and the Queen went so fast that it was all she could do to keep up with her; and still the Queen kept crying "Faster! Faster!" but Alice felt she could not go faster, though she had no breath left to say so.

The most curious part of the thing was, that the trees and other things round them never changed their places at all; however, fast Alice and the queen went, they never seemed to pass anything. "I wonder if all the things move along with us?" thought poor, puzzled Alice. And the Queen seemed to guess her thoughts, for she cried, "Faster! Don't try to talk!"

Not that Alice had any idea of doing that. She felt as if she would never be able to talk again, she was getting so much out of breath; and still the Queen cried "Faster!" and dragged her along. "Are we nearly there?" Alice managed to pant out at last.

"Nearly there?" the Queen repeated. "Why, we passed it ten minutes ago! Faster!" And they ran on for a time in silence, with the wind whistling in Alice's ears and almost blowing her hair off her head.

"Now, Now!" cried the Queen. "Faster! Faster!" And they went so fast that at last they seemed to skim through the air, hardly touching the ground with their feet, till suddenly, just as Alice was getting quite exhausted, they stopped, and she found herself sitting on the ground, breathless and giddy. The Queen said, "You may rest a little now."

Alice looked around her in great surprise. "Why, I do believe we've been under this tree the whole time! Everything's just as it was!"

"Of course it is," said the Queen; "What would you have it?" "Well, in our country," said Alice, still panting a little, "you'd generally get to somewhere else, if you ran very fast for a long time as we've been doing."

"A slow sort of country!" said the Queen. "Now, here you see, it takes all the running you can do, to keep in the same place. If you want to get somewhere else you must run at least twice as fast as that!"

We live hectic lives at a rapid pace. If we do not take the time to pray, we will get no place in our faith journey. We will find ourselves sitting among the same shallow understandings of our faith as when we first began our spiritual quest. In our accelerated lifestyles we are not really getting any place and finding very little peace where we are.

Like the queen, life tells us "Faster, faster! Don't stop to pray!" Prayer allows us to be still, to know God, to acquire His power for living.

Hectic lives burn out. Earlier in my book I mentioned the nonexistent prayer life in my marriage. My marriage went faster and faster downhill until it collapsed. We had not grown as a couple, in fifteen years, except apart. By all appearances, my wife and I looked exactly the same. We had not grown in depth or more deeply in love with each other. Outwardly, to the world's perception, we had lasted fifteen years. Outwardly beautiful, inwardly withered, we lived a rapid pace and grew very little.

Lack of prayer sidetracked me from the relationship I had in the beginning years of my marriage. A life void of prayer provided me with the opportunity to make wrong choices, major mistakes, unwise judgments. My failure to rely on God in prayer resulted in the rapidly escalating deterioration of the love between a man and woman.

In the days since I have learned the necessity and the privilege of being still and knowing God. Take time in your hectic life to pray to God, to energize your rather mundane existence. Remember, when the two men on the road to Emmaus took the time to stop walking the pathway and sat down with the Lord, they discovered Him. They talked with Him. Their hearts burned with joy. The time spent with Jesus Christ changed their time into life.

PRAYER: A TIME TO TURN ASIDE

The actors in my church have introduced me to the theatrical term *aside,* which refers to words spoken or remarks uttered by an actor who steps out of character to speak directly to the audience.

While the cast remain motionless or their dialogue has ceased, the actor who delivers the aside tells the audience what is really going on.

Prayer is our way of stepping out of character to look at ourselves, our relationship with God, and our relationships with one another. It is a time to step aside and determine where our lives are headed, to observe how we have been living. Prayer is a time to step aside into God's presence, to reevaluate our lives, and then to reenter life with a clearer perspective of God's will for us. We will be strengthened, equipped to live our lives according to His will. To allow His Spirit within us to develop our character and enrich our faith.

Prayer is the time to deliver an aside, to place ourselves before God and have an intimate dialogue with Him. It is our opportunity to say "God, can we talk?"

BEGIN YOUR LIFE RIGHT WITH PRAYER

I arrived in the residential facility for emotionally troubled and handicapped people to perform a Sunday afternoon wedding for Michele, daughter of Mary and Michael Otis, devoted members of my congregation.

Michele has been institutionalized for many of her young adult years. This was her wedding day. The service was to be performed in her room. Her parents had gathered along with a few friends and patients of the adult community.

The room was small, cluttered with all the personal belongings that one room could hold. A card table had been set up as an altar, draped in a paper party table cover and streamers. Plastic champagne glasses were on top.

Michele's intended husband, waiting outside the door, was handsomely dressed in his tuxedo, the cuffs of which lacked the tailoring of a finely fit suit. Residents of the complex crouched along the hallway.

Michele sat in a corner chair, charmingly adorned in her beautiful white wedding dress. She was loud and boisterous in happy anticipation. Heavy billows of smoke emanated from the cigarette beneath her floppy hat and veil.

Affectionately, she pointed to the piece of tattered red carpet she had placed before the makeshift altar and told me she was proud to "roll out the red carpet."

I have performed many weddings in the most elegant of

places, where families spent tens of thousands of dollars for the hundreds of guests invited. Many of those brides had spent hours in the bridal registry departments of major New York stores, following the wedding book guidelines to the finest detail.

Michele, rising from her chair, pressing her cigarette butt out in the ashtray, lifting the loosely fitted sleeve and collar back into its place, brusquely said she was ready to be married.

Her parents and a few guests gathered themselves into the center of the room as I approached the door to admit her fiancé. Just as I placed my hand on the doorknob, Michele shouted, "Wait a minute, Father!"

"What's the matter?" I inquired.

"Before you let him in, I want to do one thing! I want to get on my knees, on this floor, before I get married and thank God for the wonderful life He has given to me. He has blessed me for so long and has seen me through so many difficult times. I want to thank Him for my husband and my wedding day!"

Briefly stunned, I watched Michele drop to her knees and clasp her hands before her, and I heard her begin the words, "Our Father, who art in Heaven, hallowed be thy name . . ."

With that Mary, Michael, and I, with tears in our eyes, placed our hands on their daughter's shoulders.

What had been an imperfect setting had suddenly become perfect with the presence of God. Never before, in the hundreds of weddings I have performed, did I ever witness a bride fall to her knees in grateful thanksgiving for the gift of life God was sharing with her.

How painfully I recall this moment in a small room, in an adult resident community for the emotionally impaired. I learned how God uses simple things to confound the wise. What Michele was able to do in prayer, in beginning her married life, I was unable to do with my wife after fifteen years of marriage. My marriage lacked the perfection of prayer. I learned my lesson of the necessity of prayer to begin my life anew in this small room embraced by the love of God. I was convinced that God would see them through their rough times. Michele started her marriage right. She talked with God!

You can empower your life, celebrate the goodness of God's loving embrace, as you dialogue with Him in prayer.

FIVE EASY TIPS FOR PRAYER POWER

Our hands are usually clasped in prayer to show our devotion to God. However, your hands can become more than just an expression of prayerful submission to God.

Let your hand be a teaching tool for prayer, serving as a constant reminder of how to pray. My friend and colleague, Kenneth Harvey, minister of the McCraken Presbyterian Church in Belfast, Ireland, taught me to use my hand as a guideline for prayer. I share his illustration with you as a key to prayer—five easy steps using your fingers.

1. Your Thumb

It's the finger closest to you. Pray for those who are close to you, a spouse, a child, brother, sister, family, dear friends, people at work, neighbors. And do not forget to pray for yourself, lifting your needs, longings, and dreams to God. Lift your life to God so that He can use you to do something special in this world.

2. Your Index Finger

We use this finger to point, to give direction, to command gently, and sometimes to give harsh reproach or gentle admonishment. So we pray for those who have inspired us, those who give us direction, those who have set our feet on the pathway of new horizons: a teacher, a minister, a parent, a confidential friend, all those who have helped us to have a meaningful and fulfilling life. We need also to pray for forgiveness each time we use this finger to make harsh accusations or pass judgment rather than sharing love and understanding. So we point the finger at ourselves and know the need of our own forgiveness.

3. Your Middle Finger

Use this the tallest finger to remind you to pray for those who oversee our lives or who have dedicated their lives to the well-being and growth of others. We pray for those to whom we have entrusted the care of this world: our leaders in government and even those the Bible reminds us are our enemies, praying that those who work for peace will make decisions that will nurture our world with justice, hope, and freedom.

4. Your Fourth Finger

Those who play the piano know that this finger needs the most exercise because it is the weakest. Playing trills on the keyboard is difficult because of the weakness of this finger. In prayer then, the fourth finger reminds us to pray for those who are weak: children who need the strength of our love; elderly parents who no longer have the strength and ability to maintain their lives; the handicapped, the sick, the bereaved, the lonely, the hurting; all from whom the power of living seems depleted. Pray too for your own weakness so that God might strengthen you.

5. Your Pinky

Our smallest finger reminds us to pray for those who have less than we do: the poor, the deprived, the homeless, the aimless drifters, the untouchables, the starving, those depending upon the love of others for hope and comfort.

Add to this list. Remember, the above illustration is only a guideline to assist you in planning your daily prayer time.

After praying for all those represented by the fingers of your hand, bring your hands together and place them within God's hands, in God's loving embrace. Ask Him to receive your prayers. We know that with our lives held in His care we can "talk" to Him. We can offer up our lives to God and know that He hears us and knows our every need.

When we talk to God, we receive the power for new life.

> He speaks and listening to His voice
> New life the dead receive
> The mournful broken hearts rejoice
> The humble poor believe.[6]

God, can we talk?

Let Your Embrace Bridge Others to Christ

D usty, dirt roads. Where everyone who passes by is not a stranger. They are family, people from a small, rural village, living with bare necessities. Impoverished? No! How could they be when they are living off the resources of the earth?

Along the roadway travels a rugged-faced, dark-complexioned Greek man whose eyes reflect the serenity and contentment he has found in these hills for over seventy-eight years. He walks with a noble stride, supported by his smoothly worn cane in one hand and his arm around the shoulder of a grandson.

I watch their confident walk. In the evening of life's years, this man guides the footsteps of those who are to follow in the long tradition of family life established in the Peloponnesian area of Greece. Their village is near Olympia, where the ancient athletic competitions were held and where today the torch is lit and carried to the sponsoring country of the Olympic Games. The ruddiness, strength, and character of my Greek family who lives in the southern hills of Greece seem to confirm that the athletic strength of an Olympic competitor was bred into the people of these hills.

This is the birthplace of my grandfather. I am watching

his only living brother. His resemblance to the grandfather I called "Pa" as I was growing up is striking. I am in touch with my heritage. These shared hills bridge our lives close together and to our roots and to the love we feel for each other.

But more than being in touch with my heritage, I am in touch with God. The simple, mountain life makes the grasping of one's soul and the grasping of God's hand a possibility.

In his seventy-eight years, the farthest my uncle has ever traveled was the eleven hours north to the city of Athens. His roots are deeply embedded in this small village of 250 people. Here in Neumta Illias are buried his great-grandparents, grandparents, parents, and brother. Their graves are joined closely together in the cemetery behind their small Orthodox church. A short distance away is their neatly kept home overlooking olive and fig trees scattered among the massive mountains and valleys.

The early evening hours are greeted by the huffs of the herds of goats and sheep gently prodded on by the tap of the staff from a farmer, returning home after endless hours in the fields. Women carry dried, broken twigs in huge bundles upon their backs to replenish the firewood for cooking on their outside ovens. After sunset, men gather on the small verandas of taverns in what seems idle conversation, gradually becoming vociferous as they share family life, community needs, but very rarely world events.

They turn to me often in discussion and curiosity to hear of the world beyond the boundaries of their village line. My interpreter conveys these insights into the world beyond themselves. But mostly, their concern is about the lives of their families in America, people whom they have never met except through the exchange of letters.

Sitting here with them allows me to journey within my own soul. Here I am in touch with the essence of life.

Simplicity.

Finding refreshment through a bath in running streams. Stopping along a roadside to cup my hands and catch the trickling waters out of moss-covered rocks to splash a sweat-beaded face. The intensity of the silence, interrupted only by the sounds of rushing water over rocks and stones or the brushing of a donkey's tail swatting flies off its back.

The hours after midnight pass mysteriously slowly as the moon glows through cracks in wooden shutters. The howl of a dog in the distance incites a local dog to whine in response.

The night echoes with the unceasing crows of roosters by the hundreds in the mountain villages, defying all suggestion that they crow only at the rising of the sun. Sleep is evasive, but not because I am restless. I am in touch with life. I stay awake to soak in the essence of life here. Then peace becomes my blanket of sleep.

Dusty earthen pathways bridge my life not only to my family, but to the deeper essence of life God provides for each of us. They remind me that God has created us out of dust.

My soul is nourished here. Into that dust comes His continued creative breath. As I look towards the sky's glittering stars, the dusty trail of the Milky Way, I realize that I am a part of all that God has created.

I need not be dismayed if, in reaching for stars, I have not been able to grasp them. Here, as I stand on the top of a mountain, in the solitude of a countryside church, stagelit by moonglow, I am reminded that I can reach for the skies.

The noble man with the sturdy cane will place his arm around my shoulder as we walk the mountain paths and stop in front of small Communion altars, with memory candles and bread and wine left earlier in the day by the Greek Orthodox Priests. Here life is in communion with God and earth. The distant pathway is lit by a tiny speck of candlelight from these Communion stations.

God is near. Here life is bridged to God.

Respite will come from pausing under a fig tree. Uncle Spiros will straddle the limbs of the tree, stretching to pick a fig from the crown of the tree. The figs at the top are the earliest to ripen. They are the ones closest to the sun. And as we squeeze them, placing the succulent fruit to our lips, I remember that as we live closer to the "Son," we will bear much fruit.

My family has built me a small three-room home in this serene countryside. A few weeks there each summer are enough to mold my character and touch my soul for a lifetime.

My uncle's arm around my shoulder, we walk quietly within inexpressible love. I do not speak Greek. He knows no

English. Love is our only common bond, the bridge that unites us. The love of God whose arms are around our shoulders as we walk this road that leads to our souls.

Everyone needs an arm, an embrace, to bridge them to God. That will help them live their lives more closely to the Son.

Jesus Christ is our greatest bridge to faith. When He said, "No one comes to the Father but by me," He was suggesting that His life created a bridge to new life. Through Him we can find God.

By following the example of Jesus, we are provided with the ways to build bridges that will lead others to faith and fulfillment.

Jesus was always about building bridges, faith bridges to hope and abundant living. You can become a bridge to faith for others as the love of God is expressed through you. So many people are walking the dusty, dry pathways of life. Your embrace can bridge them to a walk that will lead beside green pastures and still waters. They will be able to rediscover their souls restored.

Ruth Liable was influential in the development of my appreciation for church worship and Christian music. Ruth was the organist of the Evangelical United Brethren Church in Newark, New Jersey, my boyhood church. After each worship service I would dash up to the organ bench and slide onto that long, smooth, shiny oak platform to be enthralled by her masterful playing.

Her eyes always welcomed me as I came to sit by her. Her broad smile, was equaled only by the intensity of the chords from the organ pipes. I could not tell whether the grandeur and majesty of the king of instruments was coming from the mounted pipes on the wall or from the loving graciousness of the one sitting next to me. I could not separate the two. To this day, many years later, she is synonymous with church music in my love for God.

During my seminary years, Ruth called and invited me to visit her. She was an elderly woman then, quite frail, yet still graceful. She walked over to a living room closet, opening the closet door to expose several large boxes on the floor. They contained the most precious folios of her neatly categorized music library.

"I never forgot how you used to sit with me on the organ bench and thrilled over the sounds from the organ. I want you to have this music, my precious music. Perhaps somewhere in your ministry you will be able to use it and keep my love for music alive."

Ruth Liable created a bridge for me, a bridge to church music. Today, I have one of the greatest choirs in New York City. Ruth is dead now, but each time the choir lifts up its voice in praise, I know that Ruth Liable's gracious spirit is with me. She was a bridge builder.

During my teen years, Burke and Alice White served as the ministerial family in our church. When they first learned of my desire to become a minister, they came to my home and presented me with a black, soft-covered New Testament, one I still treasure and use in my daily devotions.

Inscribed within were these words: "To Ron, with our hopes in you!"

They created a bridge of faith that would help lead me to an exciting ministry with Jesus Christ. They saw hope in my life and in my future.

When Burke died in his late eighties I was asked to give the eulogy at the church service to an overflowing crowd of people who had been touched by his life. My message title was "With Our Hopes in You," the hope of eternal life.

Burke and Alice believed in me and affirmed God's presence in my life. They bridged me to God's hopes and dreams. Today, my life is about building bridges.

A bridge fills a gap. It makes a pathway over a depression or an obstacle.

There are many people who have empty lives, who are filled with depression and anxiety. Many face tremendous obstacles, fears, failures, and uncertainties, and they wonder just how they will be able to overcome them. As builders of bridges to faith, we endeavor to provide a way for hurting, empty lives to overcome obstacles and barriers that have been preventing them from living joyfully. Our embrace can affirm another person. It powerfully conveys love. It can lead them to the tree of life that will bridge them closer to the "Son."

In the late sixties I was passing through the small Ohio town where a bridge expansion had collapsed, plummeting cars, twisted metal, and casualties to the swirling Ohio River below. As I glanced through the fence, temporarily erected at the ragged edge of the once-smooth roadway, the thunderous waters below surged and called up within me an intense feeling that I would dedicate my life to being a bridge builder to faith. I would provide people a way to come to Christ.

God can be the bridge in your life to faith. Your embrace can bridge others to His love. Look at the joyous truth from Deuteronomy 33:26–27:

> There is no one like the God . . .
> Who rides the heavens to help you,
> And in His excellency on the clouds.
> The eternal God *is your* refuge,
> And underneath *are* the everlasting arms.

The arms of God. Under your life and mine is that embraceable bridge to His love. Your love can build another bridge over which others can walk into a land of love.

Jesus Christ bridges our lives from death to eternal life in the kingdom of God. Only God's love can create such a bridge. And only His love within you will make you that kind of bridge builder.

EMBRACE PRAYER AND BUILD BRIDGES
OF RECONCILIATION

In their book *Back on Course,* Gavin MacCleod, captain on the television series *The Love Boat,* and Patti MacCleod tell the transforming story of their lives being bridged back together after a tragic divorce. Their remarriage is a triumphant testimony to the ability of God's love within us, bridging our lives over alienation, resentment, hatred, and suspicion. Patti says,

> In the play *Mass Appeal,* Gavin played an older priest. Just before our second wedding he repeated the priest's last speech to me: "Up to now, my need for your love and approval has kept me silent and inactive. This is the first time I've ever said

what I wanted to you. Only now is love possible. . . ." As Gavin and I made our wedding plans, I felt that now love was possible. Now that we had said yes to the Author of love we could understand what it meant to be free from earning approval and craving it. Gavin and I never had enough approval. I now feel that the closer Gavin and I become to God, the closer we will be to each other.[1]

When you bridge your life to God, becoming closer to "the Author of love," you are set free to love others, to become a bridge of love to God for them. And as you do, you will become closer to each person with whom you share the love of God.

When a life is bridged to faith, miracles happen which can defy the understanding of the secular world and mind. Patti MacCleod continues her wonderful story of the rebirth of their love by saying:

> My secular therapists had all told me to forget Gavin, let him go and get on with the business of living my life. My Christian friends and counselors were saying that the power of God could move mountains; that God is a God of restoration. The Bible says, "Ask and keep on asking; knock and keep on knocking." I had so much confidence and faith when I prayed for Gavin. It was truly a privilege. And as I prayed, a new love for him developed in me. I began to love him more. I began to forgive him more.

> The most amazing thing was happening: I began to like myself better. God was showing me I was worth something. He told me I didn't have to put myself down to justify a divorce. He showed me that in His eyes I was forgiven and righteous. I was His child, and that's what counted most. The Lord was giving me strength I hadn't had before. My prayer partner, Louise French, told me not to be discouraged. I learned that my thoughts are subject to both the Lord Jesus and to the enemy [Satan]. I wanted to think God's thoughts, so I began to pour God's Word into my mind every day.[2]

First bridging their lives to Christ and God, Patti and Gavin were able to rebuild the bridge to their marriage. Prayer was that bridge. Despite the hurt and pain that each had inflicted upon the other, that bridge of prayer developed a new love, which was not only deepened but discovered for the first time. It was a bridge that let them embrace each other in forgiveness. They found their self-worth in the embrace that bridged their lives to God. In that embrace they discovered a power and joy for living they never knew before.

As a divorced person, I believe in the tremendous power of God proclaimed by Patti and Gavin MacCleod. When two people are committed to each other in prayer, we discover that all things are possible. Their words provide hope for any of us who suffers from or has experienced the pain of rejection. There is hope for your troubled marriage or splintered relationships if you make the effort "to think God's thoughts." There is power in prayer. It will be the embrace that will bridge your lives to each other and to God. It will be the road that will lead your life to a brighter tomorrow.

Your loving embrace will bridge others to new life.

And you will like yourself better for doing it.

Each time I enter an elevator in a New York City sky-scraper, I am reminded of the level of trust necessary for step-ping into an elevator over the empty abyss of an eighty-story elevator shaft.

As we walk through life's great unknowns, we can step onto the solid foundation of Christ knowing that as a bridge to faith we can trust Him to carry us through life without possess-ing the fears of uncertainty beneath out wavering feet. For Scrip-ture says:

> To Him who is able to keep you from stumbling,
> And to present *you* faultless
> Before the presence of His glory with exceeding joy,
> To God our Savior,
> Who alone is wise,
> *Be* glory and majesty,
> Dominion and power. . . .[3]

HOW YOU CAN BE A BRIDGE TO FAITH

Following are a list of ways that you can be a bridge of faith, letting your loving embrace bring others closer to Christ.

The various dictionary definitions of bridges can help us understand how God can use our embrace to lead people to the Lord. Remember these four simple ways that will help you to bridge others to God, and you will find yourself filled with the fullness of God's love.

Be Mutually Supportive

My friend, Maxie Dunnam, former editor of *The Upper Room* devotional magazine, always signs his letters to me, "Keep on Dancing," or "Dance with the Spirit."

What a delightful way to sign his wonderful letters of faith and inspiration. Through his signature he proclaims the joy of faith shared. Keep on dancing! Within those words we discover the joy and responsibility of being mutually supportive.

One of the definitions of "bridge" is a dance term to illustrate any arch formed as people join and raise their hands. God is the choreographer of our relationships. Faith cannot be shared without our joining hands, not only with those who are strong, but to support those who are weak, lost, and uncertain about their direction. This bridge will allow those who are not clear about the next step they must take on life's pathway to keep on dancing, keep on persevering. It is the embrace that will bridge them to encouragement, motivate them to achieve, uphold them when they backslide, affirm them when they feel insecure.

It will forgive them when they make mistakes, stand by their side, supporting them when they fall.

This is what Jesus meant when He said, "I am the way, the truth and the life." His hands became mutually supportive, forming an arch, a bridge to faith. The path that would lead to God. His hands in ours form the bridge that will strengthen us. And that hand will never allow us to fall.

The church is filled with people who are mutually supportive. In it we find people who praise God with the "timbrel and dance," people whose shared love provides the support, the arch, that will hold up another life.

Sarah and I were squeezing fresh oranges for our morning breakfast on one of the weekends my children stayed with me. The half-cut oranges continually wobbled out of her hand as she tried to support them on the rotating squeezer. I placed my large, strong hand over hers, exerting pressure to extract the fresh citrus juices.

Standing next to me on a chair against the kitchen counter, while our hands were still applying pressure to the oranges, Sarah turned to me and said, "Daddy, I want you to be honest with me! Answer this question."

I marveled at her five-year-old ability to participate in such a bright and inquisitive dialogue. Both of my girls have been rather gifted and open in this aspect of relating with their parents.

"What's your question, Sarah?" I asked.

"Will you tell me the truth?"

"Sure will, honey! Won't tell you anything but the truth."

"Why did you leave my home when I was three?"

I was astounded by her forthrightness.

Promising her the truth, I began explaining as gently and clearly as possible the few details I was willing to share with her uncomprehending mind of the collapse in a marriage and the separation of her parents.

Our hands still held onto the rotating orange halves as we talked.

"Sarah, sometimes people fall out of love. We do things that hurt each other. When people don't love us anymore, it hurts. Your Mommy fell out of love with me because I didn't love her enough."

While our hands lifted another orange half to the squeezing machine, she lifted her free hand to my face, rubbed my cheek, looked up in my eyes and said, "Daddy, how could anyone not love you?"

Through her kind, compassionate, loving expression, I felt drawn to her five-year-old ability to love her Daddy, not knowing his faults, his blemishes, his mistakes, his sins, his many blunders, his insensitivities, which resulted in her parents' divorce.

All I knew was that she unequivocally loved me!

The joining of our four hands was this bridge, this arch, that led to a loving embrace between father and daughter. Her thoughts made love dance within me.

God is exactly like this. He holds one hand over ours and

places His other hand to our face. Feel the loving touch! The difference between Him and Sarah is that God sees our blemishes, knows our mistakes, is often dismayed by our sins, angry over our blunders, hurt by our insensitivity and our inability to love Him fully. And yet He places His hand to our faces. Tenderly He touches our lives, knowing us completely, and says, "How can I not love you?"

God's embrace is like Sarah's touch, bridging us to His love. Your love can be like Sarah's embrace, her simple accepting of others because she loves them. Despite all that we know about each other, we can let God's hand place within our hands the healing touch that will embrace others to Christ.

Let Your Life Fill an Empty Space

Robert Schuller of the Crystal Cathedral and television's *Hour of Power* shares with his congregation the philosophy of his caring ministry: "Find a need and fill it. Find a hurt and heal it."

Dentistry provides another great definition for a "bridge" along the same line as Dr. Schuller's thinking. Dentistry defines a bridge as a replacement of a missing tooth or teeth, supported by natural teeth adjacent to the space.

People of faith can provide the support base necessary to fill the needs of others. The Christian faith has with it the promise that we never stand alone. There is always someone who will share our heartache, who will try to lift our burden.

You can be a bridge to faith by standing by those who are hurting, alone, forgotten, troubled, confused, and uncertain about the meaning of life. For God to fill the gaps of so many empty lives, He needs the support of those who are strong in faith.

Jesus said of Peter, "Upon this rock I will build my church." Upon good faith, God can begin bridging gaps, fulfilling needs, healing hurts.

A thirty-two-year-old man named Bill came to my office, looking like one of the typical panhandlers of the city streets looking for a handout. My suspicions were immediately aroused. I set limits to the extent to which I would help him. I put limits to my love.

But I was to discover an important lesson. God would

reveal to me that there are no confines to God's love, grace, and care. God would always be there as the bridge upon which others might build their lives. Through Bill, God was going to teach me a lesson on being a bridge builder, on embracing him and providing a bridge that would lead to God's love

Bill had been drifting in New York for a few days, penniless. This was his first visit to the Big Apple, so he claimed. For several months he was visiting relatives in Connecticut and now was on his way back to his wife and children in North Carolina. He had been without food for several days. I had heard this familiar story countless times. I would not be made a "sucker." Further limits were set to my love for him. It was the all-too-familiar manipulation that street drifters pull on staff people at churches.

Then a brilliant thought illuminated my mind. If I could get into his wallet, I might learn that his story was credible. Or I would know that my suspicions were correct.

"Do you have a picture of your wife and children?" I asked.

With a broadening smile and great pride, he opened his wallet, out of which dropped the long plastic enclosures of eight or ten pictures of his family. The joy of their lives glittered in his eyes. Having his wallet in my possession gave me the opportunity to browse through for any evidence that would discredit him.

I hit the jackpot!

An identification card with the heading "Connecticut Probation Office," complete with identification number and the current date. Staring into my face was a parolee. I knew now that he was not telling me the truth.

"You served time in prison?" I suspiciously inquired of him. Hesitating in embarrassment he unfolded the details that led to his arrest. Living in Connecticut with a cousin, he was in the car of his relative who was committing a robbery at a local small food chain. Though Bill didn't know what his cousin was doing, both men were arrested.

"It was my first offense. I have no previous record."

He was not sentenced, but placed under probation and required to return to his family in North Carolina. No interstate transportation was provided. His hitchhiking venture brought him now to New York.

What a totally prefabricated story, I thought. *You're a fool, Cadmus, if you fall for this one.* I continued to set the limits to my caring love. A bridge builder I was not.

Noticing a phone number and name of his probation officer, I made a mental image of it.

"Wait a minute, Bill," I said, as I walked to another office to call the probation officer in Connecticut. I told Bill I was checking to see if we had any food in our supply closet.

When I reached the probation officer, I introduced myself as a minister in New York City inquiring about this aimless drifter named Bill. Providing his identification number, I was curious to know if she knew of this case and if she could verify the information that Bill shared with me.

He had told me the truth! I was shocked. And quite humiliated.

"Ron, if you and your church can help Bill in any way to return to his family in North Carolina, I will be deeply grateful! We could only give him a few dollars. The rest of the arrangements were up to him."

I peered through the slightly opened office door to see Bill quietly waiting for me in the church lobby. I asked God to forgive me my suspicions, to help me take the limits off my love. Bill and I began to interact with each other, and the discovery of being a bridge builder to the embraceable love of God became more and more important.

"Bill, get your coat and come with me."

We went to the Port Authority bus terminal a few blocks from the church and walked up to the Trailway bus ticket agent. In my wallet, my finger tips grabbed the little green American Express card.

"Sir, this wonderful young man needs a one-way ticket to Morgantown, North Carolina."

Disbelief welled up in Bill's eyes; underneath was complete joy.

He was going home. Someone purchased a ticket for his trip home.

He picked up the ticket and walked to the bus platform.

We had some time to wait. A few greasy hot dogs satisfied his stomach. A Coke quenched his thirst.

Up until this time we had not spoken about the faith nor the church. I felt that before he boarded the bus I needed to share with him the love of Christ, not only in my action of purchasing a ticket, but in witnessing about the embraceable love of God that was now bridging him to his home. I had nothing to lose. This was possibly the first and last visit we would ever have.

"Bill, do you belong to a church?"

"Yes, I attend a small Baptist church in Morgantown."

Putting my arms around his shoulder, I asked, "Do you believe that God loves you, and that there are people who care for you? Do you believe that God wants you to live a good life? Make right choices? Build a strong faith? Love your wonderful family? Be a good father and husband?"

Tears flowed down his cheeks onto his quivering lips.

We prayed.

We hugged each other.

Bill's bus arrived. He was going home. We watched each other until the bus was out of sight. The experience became a memory as quickly as it had become a miracle.

Our loving embrace can build a bridge in empty lives, lost lives, in the hearts of people trying to find their way back home to themselves and to God.

Never expecting to hear from him, I was going through the office mail one day when I noticed a return address from Morgantown, North Carolina. It read:

> I hope this letter finds you doing well. I made it home the next day at 1:15. I want to thank you and the good Lord for your help. I really appreciate what you have done for me, with the ticket and money. My wife couldn't believe it when I explained the help you have given me—a total stranger.
>
> We both prayed and thanked the Lord for making a great thing happen and for people like you. I am working hard on living the way the Lord wants me to. I have been trying real hard every day—seeking employment. I got a few prospects. As soon as I get a job I will send you a payment.
>
> I have seen a probation officer here but my paper work hasn't arrived yet. But I'll have to report to them soon. I

hope to be working before then. I let my wife write a few lines now.

Dear Rev. Cadmus,

I am Bill's wife, Jean. I am writing to thank you for helping my husband get home to me. I really needed him. I am very happy he is home safe. Bill said we will always have a good friend in New York City. We will keep in touch with you. Write soon.

Your friends, . . .

God teaches us that there are no limits to His love, His embraceable love that will bridge people back to an understanding of what His love is for them. Through Bill I learned that there should be no limits to my love, that through all of our lives, we can stand alongside people, as we grow to trust and love them, bridging the gaps in their empty lives.

Through Bill I learned about that embraceable love of God, who through Jesus Christ, His Son, paid the price that would lead us back home to the kingdom of God. God and Jesus Christ will always stand at your side, bridging your life to faith.

HELP PEOPLE TO SEE THAT THEY ARE GOD'S CHILDREN

Your embrace can help people see their lives in a new way.

When Jesus came to the blind man who so desperately wanted to be healed, our Lord asked a most significant question: "What do you want?"

The blind man cried, "I want to see!"

In anatomy, the ridge or upper line of the nose is called a "bridge." The bridge of the nose. For those who wear eyeglasses, two little prongs are called the bridge. They rest on the nose, providing the support for the glasses.

As a bridge to faith, you can provide the support that will allow people to perceive themselves clearly as God's children, as significant, worthwhile individuals. They can begin to see

Christ within their lives. They can see that power for living comes from Christ.

Matthew 6:22–24 says, "The lamp of the body is the eye. If therefore your eye is good, your whole body will be full of light. But if your eye is bad, your whole body will be full of darkness."

Christ is the bridge that gives us a clear perspective on the abundant life we can have. When we see him as the light of our world, our whole body will be full of new life.

Your loving embrace can become the bridge through which others can clearly see that they are loved.

Mary Castiglia, an elder of my congregation and member of the governing body of the Collegiate Church, vibrantly allowed the Lord to open her eyes, to use her life as a bridge so that others might see God's love for them more clearly.

When we initiated the Prison Fellowship Ministry at our local congregation in relationship to Chuck Colson's Prison Fellowship, Mary had strong, justified feelings against this program. She was vehemently opposed to it. Several undercover New York City policemen are members of our congregation. For many the philosophy about criminals in New York is to "lock them up and throw away the key," certainly an attitude remote from Christ's mandate to set the prisoner free.

Mary was still dealing with a great deal of personal pain and hurt from the murder of her brother during a robbery of his home. "A ministry to prisoners in my church! Never!" In fact, she was able to significantly sway the Board to suspicion of our newly developed mission to inmates and their families.

A referral was made one day to my office regarding an unwed mother. The father of her infant child was in prison. The family was on welfare and had this new baby, who was allergic to breast milk. A special formula was needed to nourish its frail life. Welfare could not provide all the money for the huge quantity of special formula needed in the year ahead.

I called Mary, a head nurse at Lenox Hill Hospital in Manhattan, about whether we would be able to get the formula from the hospital pediatrics department. After briefly investigating it, she told me that the milk was unavailable.

There was nothing she could do.

I felt she was completely uninterested—until a phone call several days later.

"Ron, I've been thinking and praying about this young woman and her baby. I can't escape thoughts of them. I want to give you a check for a year's supply of formula."

I was deeply moved by the way the Lord was embracing Mary, herself, with the bridge that was allowing her to perceive God's will for her life in a new way. That allowed her to perceive the urgent needs of the other. Mary was becoming a bridge builder.

"I want to give this money and pray that it might be the first step, after all these years, to begin my own forgiveness of the one who took my brother's life."

Nothing else but the embraceable love of God could have allowed Mary to embrace others and bridge them to the love of God. Since that wonderful day Mary and her family have helped other inmates and their families rehabilitate themselves. A quick call to her with an emergency need releases her compassionate love and her generous giving to help others to take the first step onto the pathway of new life.

When I saw Mary one day after church move across the church aisle to greet a newly released parolee who had been one of the conspirators in the Brink's robbery, embracing him with a hug and a kiss and the extended hand of Christian fellowship, I knew that God had been a bridge within Mary's life. She allowed God to open her eyes. And as Matthew said, "if your eye is good, your whole body will be full of light." Mary was radiating the light and love of Jesus Christ. God's love first embraced her. Then she became a bridge that led an inmate and his family to the love of God. She loved them into the fellowship of the church.

DON'T BE AFRAID TO ASK PEOPLE FOR HELP

Often, we cannot handle our own problems. But many people are afraid to ask for help.

Our last bridge is taken from the pool hall, the billiard table, where we find a clever instrument called a bridge. Any pool shark will know that there are difficult shots to be made on the felt table top. Our awkward position makes the degree of the angle or the shot to be made, virtually impossible without the use of the bridge.

This special bridge is designed to help us when our shot is impossible to make. At the end of the long stick there is a ridged piece of metal in the formation of the top of your knuckles if you make a fist. You place the bridge on the table and upon one of the notches in the bridge you place the cue.

This bridge supports your cue for the difficult shot. Without it, chances are you would "scratch" the ball, completely missing the shot.

Problems in life present us with the same difficulties. You need a support base, a community of faith, the embraceable arms of a friend to help you.

And you need not, must not be afraid to ask for that help.

After all, like the bridge in pool, the Christian has been designed to offer the same support.

The greatest bridge of faith is the cross upon which Christ has taken our sin, the cross through which we are forgiven.

Ask Him for guidance and help, and He will create within you a bridge that will lead to God. "Come unto me and I will give you rest." Place your life upon Christ, and He will bridge you to new life! The psalmist said, "Cast thy burden upon the Lord, and He shall sustain thee. He never will suffer the righteous to fall: He is at the right hand. Thy mercy, Lord, is great."

Cast your life upon the Lord. Rest it upon Him, this Bridge to God. As the cue is stabilized on the ridge of the bridge, your life is sustained and stabilized on the outstretched arms of Jesus Christ, those arms which envelope you in His loving embrace. Those arms were once stretched out upon the cross, upon which rests your whole life. And as God does this for you, you will discover how to be a bridge on whom others might find support and encouragement.

Charles Dickens' novel *Nicholas Nickleby* reveals to us the comfort and joy that comes from allowing your embrace to bridge others to God.

"If it wasn't for you I'd die," says young Smike to Nicholas Nickleby.

These are words of one dependent upon another for life.

This story begins in Devonshire. The Nickleby family, who has recently suffered the death of their husband and father, leaves London where they depend upon the mercy of their only living relative, Ralph Nickleby, uncle of Nicholas.

Ralph Nickleby helps the family grudgingly and places many conditions on his assistance. He finds young Nicholas a job at a school for boys in Yorkshire. Here Nicholas meets Smike among the forty other boys who are mistreated, pale with haggard faces, lonely, and bony. They look like old men, all darkened with the pain of suffering.

Smike is nineteen years old, crippled, bent over with lameness, and dressed in ragged garments he has long since outgrown.

As a small child he was abandoned by his father, who conceived him out of wedlock. Sometime after the abandonment, the father came inquiring about his son but was told that his child had died. In reality, however, he had been secretly given away to this boys' school.

Nicholas discovers in Smike a frightened young man, cold and despairing. He is riddled by the fears and scars of his past, as he remembers being confined to a dark attic room when he was abandoned as a child. His life is full of pain and fear. It is difficult for him to face the possibility of his death in a world in which he is neglected and unloved.

These fears are shared with Nicholas, Smike's only bridge to comfort and hope.

"I was with another young boy named Sorker who died. I was with him at the end. He asked for me. But who will I ask for? Who will be with me when I die?" asks Smike.

Hopeless, he claims there is no purpose and hope left in life to which Nicholas offers a reassuring claim: "There is always hope!"

"Is there?" Smike says, "for an *outcast?* A person cast out, rejected, forsaken—this homeless one!"

And Nicholas, feeling the pain and fear of young Smike, begins a relationship that is built into a bridge of faith, that will add a strength and hope for a young cripple rejected by the world.

"Except for Nicholas, I die," claims Smike. He finds hope in one who has begun carrying him through his difficult ordeals.

Unable to handle the horrors of the mistreatment by the schoolmaster, Smike becomes a runaway, only to be caught and whipped. Nicholas intercedes on behalf of young Smike, turning upon the villainous schoolmaster with his own cane, and carries crippled Smike away from the school, both never to return again. They become inseparable. Smike finds hope through one who becomes a bridge to faith. His new sense of security in a frightening world is expressed when he says of Nicholas, "You are home to me." Isn't that beautiful? Your life and love providing the security of a home for someone else.

As Dickens unfolds the plot, we discover that Smike is the abandoned son of the wealthy, aristocratic Ralph Nickleby.

In the uncovering of the tragic story of his abandonment, Smike reveals his recurrent nightmares of the dark attic room where he was hidden away from public speculation and ridicule. He says "Till now, I have not known two days together when I haven't been afraid."

It is Nicholas' faithful love that begins breaking the fear that cripples Smike.

Nicholas becomes his only friend, one for whom he says, "I would lay down my life." Finally succumbing to his weakened bodily sickness Smike dies in the place where he has found his greatest security—in the arms of Nicholas Nickleby. His greatest fear that no one will be there when he dies never materializes. Nicholas' arms are the caring embrace that bridges Smike to love and faith.

Ralph Nickleby's discovery of the true identity of his abandoned son, whom he himself has called a social outcast, is a burden of guilt too heavy for him. In the same dark attic room where the child Smike had been confined, Ralph begins a soliloquy of remorse and guilt and realizes he has forfeited the fullness of living because of a selfishness that prevented him from becoming a bridge to faith. Looking around the room he says,

"Had he grown up here, might we have been a comfort to each other? And might I have been a different man?"

In guilt and shame, in the dark attic room, Ralph Nickleby hangs himself.

The closing scene of the play based on Dickens' novel has the full cast of characters gathered on the stage on Christmas Eve. Nicholas, newly and happily married, finds fulfillment and joy in his new life and in the joy of the season. Gathered in merriment the cast sings a great Christmas carol around which Dickens lifts up the theme of joy and comfort that comes from allowing our embrace to bridge others to God, resulting in our own joy and fulfillment:

> Now to the Lord sing praises,
> All you within this place,
> And with true love and brotherhood
> Each other now embrace.[4]

While the cast sings merrily, Nicholas suddenly becomes immobilized as he glances center stage. His eyes fall upon a young cripple, who sits dejected, frightened, alone on this Christmas Eve.

Nicholas moves away from the merry crowd and slowly approaches the crippled boy, the newly found outcast.

Deep within his heart is the desire to reach out to touch him. His hand hesitantly moves toward the boy, but he cannot touch him. Can he commit himself so completely again? Deeper still within him is the hesitating fear of becoming emotionally involved with one who is outcast on the dusty, dry, frightening road of life.

Nicholas looks at the boy. He has given so much to Smike. Can he again go through the pain of caring again for one who will demand all of his love?

He moves away.

His wife sees the torment of his conflict and indecision, of the fear of committing himself again to love's call.

Then the chorus begins to sing more loudly, "And with true love and brotherhood, each other now embrace."

He turns to the new Smike. He can't leave him. He touches him. A pale, haggard face, filled with the darkness of suffering looks up into his eyes. Nicholas reaches down and swings the boy into the cradle of his caring embrace, and the chorus resounds with a triumphant "tidings of comfort and joy, comfort and joy."

And there is the truth that underlies the loving embrace, your embrace that will bridge others to God. Comfort and joy, contentment and serenity come from being a bridge to faith, by bearing upon your life the needs of others who walk aimlessly and frightfully along dusty pathways.

Such a joy the father of Smike did not know. Before he hangs himself he says, "Would we have been a comfort to each other had we cared for each other?"

But God knows this joy. For when Christ was hung on the cross, it was God's way of embracing us all with a love that would bridge our lives to Him.

Being a bridge to faith will give you comfort and joy. If you are a bridge, others will find comfort and joy, strength and security as you lift them closer to the "Son." As Smike said to Nicholas, "You are home to me," your loving embrace of those you meet will bring them home to faith and to God.

When Christ becomes our bridge to faith, we find that home.

Have you set limits to how far you will go in loving other people? Is there someone in your life who needs you to stand by his side, sharing with him acceptance and your loving support? A forgiving word? Let God use your embrace as a bridge that will lead him to Christ.

> I've found a Friend, O Such a Friend!
> He loved me ere I knew him;
> He drew me with the cords of love.
> And thus He bound me to Him.
> And round my heart still closely twine
> Those ties which naught can sever,
> For I am His, and He is mine,
> Forever and forever.

The embrace of our Friend, Jesus Christ that will forever bridge us to God, to the kingdom. And it is there that we will affirm

God, you are home to me!

Let your embrace bridge others to that home.

CHAPTER 15

No Grave Doubts About Easter

For every hour and every moment thousands of men leave life on this earth, and their souls appear before God. And how many of them depart in solitude, unknown, sad, dejected, that no one mourns for them or even knows whether they have lived or not.

—Fyordor Dostoyevsky, *The Brothers Karamazov*

While the graveside mourners walked solemnly back to their cars, the immediate family members remained in quiet solitude and grief beside the bronze casket, which shimmered as it reflected the rays of sunlight dancing through the leaves overhead. Silent hugs were filled with caring love. The remains of a loved one lay isolated in the empty space where moments earlier 150 people offered their final respects to a beloved man of my congregation.

The cars edged their way along the small winding path, leaving the cemetery. The union workers, in their dirt encrusted work clothes, seemed callously disengaged from the broken hearts which only seconds before had gathered in a circle of love.

I'm always bothered by the exchange of money between the funeral directors and the union workers as if this last act of respect for one of earth's children, laying a body decently in earth's last domain, calls for a tip.

The waving hands of a funeral director, summoned me from across the grounds. Walking toward the other gravesite, I found myself standing before a gray, compressed cardboard casket. The unknown person in this casket was a state case, no family, unnoticed while alive and alienated even in death. I was asked to say a brief prayer.

This person was one of the thousands who "depart in solitude, unknown, sad, dejected, that no one mourns for them or even knows whether they have lived or not."

But to God, this magnified moment of dejection, was filled with the truth that He would never leave any of us desolate. We need have no grave doubts about the fact that God's loving embrace was wrapped around this moment of loneliness. Such a thought made this moment a bit more humane and shed a spirit of light and promise on this soul now appearing before God.

To the believer in Jesus Christ, God made a wonderful promise regarding His loving embrace. Whoever believes in Him, whether living or dead, will have eternal life. No grave! A hole in the ground, earth's last cold embrace, would gain no possessive claim or rights over any of God's faithful children.

Have no grave doubts. God intends for you to have, not a grave, but the warm, loving embrace of His kingdom. This is the power of the cross. It is the promise of Easter. Such a truth God yearns for each of us to embrace.

Cling to God's embrace, and you will find your life enveloped in eternal life.

It is at the cross, emblazoned now in glory before an empty tomb, that we find life's greatest power for living, and life's most loving embrace. Through the cross we find God's willingness to make life significantly meaningful.

We can never guess its secret power, or grasp it for that matter, until we find ourselves possessors of it by letting the power of God assume a presence of faith within our lives.

> Come down, O Love divine,
> Seek thou this soul of mine,
> And visit it with thine own ardor glowing;
> O Comforter, draw near,
> Within my heart appear,
> And kindle it, thy holy flame bestowing. . . .
>
> And so the yearning strong,
> With which the soul will long,
> Shall far outpass the power of human telling;
> For none can guess its grace,
> Till he become the place
> Wherein the Holy Spirit makes his dwelling.

Have no grave doubts about this fact. Ask God to come into your life and you will find the answer to life's greatest power for living: God Himself within you, loving you, embracing you.

Epictetus gives this statement of the mythical god Jupiter: "If it had been possible to make your body and your property free from liability to injury, I would have done so. As this could not be I have given you a small portion of myself."

The difference between Jesus Christ and this mythical god was that God found it possible to give more than a portion of Himself. He gave His whole life so that we might have new life. Have no grave doubts about this one truth. In Christ, God has given to you eternal life.

HAVE NO GRAVE DOUBTS ABOUT EASTER

Christ rose from the dead that we might have everlasting life. Joseph of Arimathea illustrates to us God's intention that we were never meant to have a tomb. We should not have any "grave" doubts about God's Easter proclamation that we would have everlasting life through Christ.

> When evening had come, there came a rich man from Arimathaea, named Joseph, who himself had also become a disciple

of Jesus. This man went to Pilate and asked for the body of Jesus. Then Pilate commanded the body to be given to him. And when Joseph had taken the body, he wrapped it in a clean linen cloth, and laid it in his new tomb which he had hewn out of the rock; and he rolled a large stone against the door of the tomb, and departed.[1]

This critical passage reveals to Christ's faithful followers God's plan for their lives. Joseph of Arimathea laid Christ, not only in a tomb hewn out of rock, but in *his own* tomb, a tomb he had hewn for himself.

What happened in that tomb removes all grave doubts about God's ability to give to his children eternal life. Freshly hewn. Unused. Its purpose? To provide God's new message of faith. We would never know the confinement of the grave.

Christ's burial there and the Easter proclamation three days later affirmed His own purpose of the Incarnation, his birth within our lives. Within Christ's birth we discover God's Easter plan!

Have no grave doubts about Easter. Christ was born, lived, crucified, and risen from the dead so that we might rise with Him and have new life.

> Good Christians now rejoice,
> With heart and soul and voice;
> Now ye need not fear the grave;
> Jesus Christ was born to save!
> Calls you one and calls you all,
> To gain his everlasting hall.
> Christ was born to save.

The empty tomb that Joseph of Arimathaea made for himself was never to be used by him.

Christ took his place.

He entered the tomb. And if it was God's intention that Christ not stay there, then we too must have no grave doubts about Easter. We need not fear the grave as the end of our earthly life. Death for the believer is a transition to new life.

The truth of the tomb is this. We were not meant to have a tomb. We were meant to have a home in God's Kingdom. We have no grave doubts about this nor any false illusions about the garden scene on Easter morning.

The disciples were in a great state of despair after the death of Jesus because they had forgotten the scriptural proclamation that after three days he would rise from the dead. They did not believe what the prophets had said. They faced Easter with many "grave" doubts.

We find our faith enhanced by their doubting. To us has been revealed the reason for the disciples' doubt, fear, and loss of faith and hope. We need not succumb to their doubts about the grave. Scripture has revealed the risen Christ, and therefore we need not have any grave doubts about Easter.

A tour of Universal Movie Studios in Burbank, California, provided me with an interesting insight into one of Hollywood's greatest heroes, John Wayne.

The tour guide escorted our group through some of the local sets used for filming many of John Wayne's famous Western movies. As the tram wound its way through several of the ghost lots, it came to a halt in front of a local saloon which had often been used for Wayne's famous struts through the swinging saloon doors.

The tumbleweed props were still strewn about the porch. All of us felt the presence of John Wayne.

Our guide asked if we noticed anything unusual about the saloon storefront.

With curiosity aroused, seventy-five pair of tourist eyes on the tram surveyed the set without noting a hint of anything peculiar.

Then the illusion was revealed. The door of the saloon was constructed smaller than the standard eighty inches so that when John Wayne was filmed pushing his way through the squeaking doors, he would appear larger than reality to help enhance his image and character as one of America's giant stars of the screen.

The door's reduced size created an illusion, making John Wayne to appear larger than reality. This simple fact burst all of our illusions regarding those whom we make our heroes.

But have no grave doubts about this fact of faith.

When the women stood in front of the tomb on Sunday morning, there was no false illusion about the tomb's open door.

The triumphant power of God had raised Christ from the dead. The empty tomb, the resurrected Jesus Christ, was no illusion created by biblical writers to give credibility to the character of Jesus.

It was the risen Christ whom Mary encountered in the garden, and who, despite all grave doubts about Easter, stood before her, magnifying God's promise of eternal life. Jesus stood before her as life magnified. Her words dispersed the clouds of doubt and are heralded to this day.

"I have seen the Lord! He is risen!"

She was standing in the presence of life's greatest power for living. Mary was held in the loving embrace of God.

The resurrected Lord was proof enough that He had come that we might have eternal life. If there were grave doubts about it prior to this moment, the resurrection appearance disputed them.

Belief in Easter is belief in the abundant power of faith for living. And like Mary we too stand before Christ. The empty tomb is no illusion, no contrived story to tell an interesting tale, in the words of Shakespeare, "told by an idiot."

It is faith in the resurrection that has offered to countless people the promise of hope. Emil Brunner, in his book *The Great Invitation,* tells of this powerful faith for living. Emil Brunner introduces us to a crowd of forty thousand people who were gathered in a stadium for an Easter Sunday service. The service was being held in a sports stadium in one of the world's communist countries. Here the grace and power of God triumphing over Communism were to be displayed.

Dispersed through the stadium and seated on the platform were uniformed Communist officers, forces whose purpose was to subvert any public affirmation of faith. For over three hours this massed congregation sat listening to a Communist propaganda attempt to suppress any infiltration of religious thought at this gathering.

A clergyman seated on the dais asked the political leaders if he might share just four words with his fellow Christians. After some whispered discussion, they relinquished the podium to the clergyman. "After all," they said, "what can be said in four words?"

The minister stood before the hushed crowd of forty thousand longing hearts intent on hearing what their shepherd would proclaim to them. Gaining his courage, undergirded by the power of the Spirit, he uttered the four words that would turn the stadium into a canyon echoing with the gospel truth:

"Jesus Christ is risen!"

With resounding fervor, forty thousand people of the faith rose to their feet and said,

"Christ is risen, indeed!"

Echoing faith embraced forty thousand people in God's love. That same faith embraces the world today.

In January 1985 the news media reported the demolition of the Church of the Reconciliation in East Berlin.

The windows of this church, located next to the wall that divided the East from the West, provided many people a means of escape to freedom. The church's very name symbolized the hope of restoration to freedom and new life.

Our television screens showed us the destruction of the city's only hope. It was demolished by the Communist regime, which felt the church obstructed a clear line of fire and threatened border security. With its destruction we saw the death of the soul of the city.

And yet Revelation tells us, "there is no need of the temple for I shall be in the midst of them."

The presence of the resurrected Christ in this world affirms that Christ will still suffer and continually give His life for the renewal of hope in despairing lives. No demolition of a church by human hands would ever be able to quiet the power of faith and God within this world. For Christ is risen indeed! Victory over death is His. He is a light no darkness will ever distinguish, an embrace which can never be unfolded.

The story of Lazarus rising from the dead shows us how God's love embraces us. The shroud of death was unwrapped by the embrace of love. Lazarus knew the power of love's embrace.

When Jesus received the message from Mary and Martha, Lazarus' sisters, that his "dear friend was sick," He did not leave the place where He and his disciples had gathered.

In fact, He stayed away two more days. How insensitive His lack of response must have appeared to Mary and Martha. Their brother was dying. Jesus apparently did not care.

Two days later Jesus returns to Judea's small town of Bethany, confronting the outrage of two angry sisters. Can you imagine the disbelief of the disciples when they heard Jesus' words: "Lazarus has died, and I am glad that I was not there."

Often we hear only what we want to hear. Occasionally, people will react to statements they hear in messages I deliver. A negative reception will often close people down to hearing what Paul Harvey says is "the rest of the story."

So, when Jesus said, "Lazarus has died, and I am glad that I was not there," the disciples' disbelief could have very well resulted in their not hearing the words that followed: "Lazarus is dead, and I am glad for your sakes that I was not there, that you may believe."[2]

Believe what?

Jesus' ability to raise someone from the dead?

No!

Scripture has already revealed to us Christ's power to raise people from the dead.

His delay was made to help us observe what the power of faith can do for one who possesses life's greatest power for living, for the one who is embraced by faith.

Jesus was greeted by an irate sister. He was greeted by no passive or subdued sentimentality. "If you had been here, my brother would not have died!"

These were harsh words of accusation! Martha felt Jesus had been disloyal. "If you had been here, *my brother would not have died!*" Martha was *enraged*.

But Jesus knew the depth and quality of Lazarus' faith, a faith that even his disciples did not possess.

Did not Jesus say that this experience was for their sake so that they might believe?

Jesus consoled Martha, promising that Lazarus would live, not by any miracle-producing ability of His or God's but by the miracle-producing ability that results from real faith that is embraced by God's love. In Lazarus we see real faith, God-sized faith, faith that would move mountains and even break open the grave.

The disciples, Mary, and Martha lacked this powerful faith so necessary to receive abundant and eternal life. As we recall this story we find our faith called into question.

"I am the resurrection and the life. Whoever believes in Me will live. Martha, do you believe this?"

He asks the same question of you and me today. Our whole belief system is called into question as we hear Jesus Christ ask us if we believe that He, and no one else, is the resurrection and the life.

When Martha finally emerged from the kitchen, after having tried to avoid the Savior for as long as she could, Jesus found Himself confronted with a second angry sister.

Jesus still knew the secret that had yet to be revealed to His followers, that development of their faith was the reason He had delayed his return until after Lazarus' death.

"Where have they laid him?" Jesus asked.

"Come and see." In front of the tomb, Jesus wept. He wept not for the loss of his dear friend. He wept over the fact that here, buried in this tomb, was finally the one who would prove that a life lived in faith would produce miracles. What we discover in Lazarus is what the Lord hopes for all of us—unwavering faith.

What was now about to happen would give witness to the power of faith. Yes, Jesus could have kept Lazarus from dying had He arrived immediately after He received the urgent message to return to Bethany.

It was not Jesus who would bring Lazarus back to life. It was faith *in* Jesus that would restore him.

With fearful uncertainty, the friends of Lazarus removed the stone from the tomb entrance.

Again the underlying grave doubts about God's ability are seen in Martha's fear of uncovering the odor that would seep from the tomb off a body that had decayed for four days.

A gentle guarantee and reminder were conveyed to her again by Jesus. "Did I not tell you that if you would believe you would see the glory of God?"

And he cried with a loud voice, "Lazarus, come out!"

The man who had been dead came out, with his hands and feet bound with bandages and his face wrapped with a cloth.

When Lazarus was set free he stood before them wrapped—embraced—by God's love.

In Lazarus the truth of faith was finally revealed. The faithful will not be confined to a grave.

This biblical account was not to bear witness to Christ's ability to perform miracles. Rather, it demonstrates the power of faith. And so, I ask the same question: "Do you believe this?"

Your answer will measure the power of your faith.

If you have such a deep, unwavering faith as Lazarus, you will see life from God's perspective. "Didn't I tell you that you would see God's glory if you believe?"

Belief in this loving embrace of God will give to you the strength you need for living life creatively and bountifully. How is this made possible for you? Not only by being embraced in God's love. It happens when you embrace God's love. As you reach out to be enclosed in the arms of such affection, you will discover a love that will always be with you, the ever-present promise, "I will always be with you."

A colleague of mine introduced me to Groucho Marx's *Hello, I Must Be Going*. In this autobiography Marx offers a commentary on our times that makes us realize that we cannot rely on life itself for strength and power for living. We need God's loving embrace.

Groucho tells us,

> Loved ones die and we are not sure we
> ever got to know them. Hello, I must be going.

> Children are born to us, grow up in our homes
> and in their own way say, "Hello, I must be going."

> A marriage falters and fails.
> Hello, I must be going.

> A promising employee is lured away by the
> competition.
> Hello, I must be going.

> Lonely people look for Mr. or Mrs. Goodbar.
> Hello, I must be going.

> People waste away in nursing homes.
> A youth group visits once a year at Christmas.

Hello, I must be going.

Nervous mortgage bankers look at a decaying
neighborhood,
Hello, I must be going.

A busy executive father swings by the house.
Hello, I must be going.

A physician, drained and too overworked to remain
human, makes his rounds.
Hello, I must be going.

Human beings are stored away in prisons and
mental hospitals where visits are always,
Hello, I must be going.[3]

Have no grave doubts about the love God has for you. His is an embrace that will never let you go. He is within your heart, in your everyday experience of living.
Renewing,
Redeeming,
Forgiving, with grace abounding to overflowing. His love will lift you. His loving embrace will release new life in you. His touch will comfort and restore you.

◘   E P I L O G U E   ◘

As God's Love Embraces you, there is only one ending to con-
clude in the telling of His story of Grace. The old self passes
away. New Life is the only alternative and joy forever embracing you with His grace.

   the beginning. . . .
        the deepening of faith
           the nurturing of the soul
              the wounds healed
                ransomed
                  healed
                    restored
                      forgiven
                        the preface. . . .

the end of this story climaxes at the essence of the gift of
grace—the beginning. . . .

And so, there comes a point when the author remains silent in
the face of things eternal; in the awesome promise of God's love
and embrace. Toby and Barb Waldowski, my close and personal
friends from the Crystal Cathedral in California, capture what I
have so meagerly expressed in my own words, the embrace that
leads to forgiveness, new life. To the beginning.

> How can I repay You
> How can I express to You my gratitude
> Remember our first meeting
> The crowd the stones the cheating
> The disgraceful mood
> But You were so unbending
> So calm and self-assured
> Amid the noisy rush
> I looked into Your eyes
> You looked inside my heart
> And brought a quiet hush

Suddenly the horror
The raucous accusations
Seemed so far away
My mind seemed to be spinning
A whirlwind of conflicting
Contradicting haze
You spoke with such compassion
My child you are forgiven
Go and sin no more
I knew that it was true
Who was this awesome Man
I'd never seen before

Now I've been born again
I've never been the same
Since then because of You
My dignity's restored
Some say You are the Lord
I know it's really true
As long as I have life and breath
I won't forget the moment
When You touched my soul
And light came bursting through
There's no way to repay
There's nothing I can say
I give my life to You

Since that day You freed me
I've never left Your presence
You're a part of me
All my old temptations
By Your liberation have begun to flee
I know You're something special
Are You the Holy One
That we've long waited for?
Wherever You've come from
Oh Jesus You're the One
I love forevermore[1]

His look inside your heart! A quiet hush! . . . this is the beginning! Of love forevermore.